My Favorite Color is YELLOW

CHIPOTLE

a poetic memoir by **Kayla Eloise**

MY FAVORITE COLOR IS YELLOW

by Kayla Eloise

my favorite color is yellow

Second Print (2026 Live Revision)

ISBN: 979-8-218-96709-3
Published by Kayla Kreates
www.kaylakreates.com
Pittsburgh, PA

Editor & Illustrator: Kayla Eloise Milliones

TABLE OF CONTENTS

preface	3
happy poems	5
negative c h e m i s t r y	7
sometimes ...	9
tnt: trials and tribulations	11
the blues	13
ataxia	15
spinning	17
filled with loss	19
every mourning ,	21
just breathe	23
i'm good	25
mutiny of the mind	27
black hole	29
catch me before i fall	31
hues	33
shaped by the lies I was told	35
my mother's shoes	37
my dearest king,	39
"don't cry over spilled milk"	41
she cries	43
hydrate daily	45
as far as it depends on me	47
commonality	49
gravity	51
my eternal friend	53
cause and affect	55
reality check	57
a pantoum of affirmation	59
strong	61
marigold	63
set me free	65
Hood Life	71

preface

They always say you should check on your strong friends too. My friends and family would describe me as an overall optimistic, confident, and charismatic person. But during my early twenties, the pressures of becoming an adult, being in a completely new environment, and identifying childhood traumas weighed on me heavily. What at first seemed to be seasonal depression quickly spiraled into a traumatic and crippling case of anxiety that nearly ended in suicide.

All the while, no one around me knew what I was going through. I continued to portray the charismatic person that everyone was familiar with, in fear of “ruining the mood.” So I held it in, often writing poems when the weight of it all became too much to bear. I decided to share these writings because there were times that I couldn’t articulate what I was experiencing until I wrote it down. There were many times in which I felt alone, although I actually was not. It wasn't until I slowed down and reflected on my experiences that I realized the reality of it all. If by chance these poems might provide some sort of solace even to just one person going through a similar situation, I would be glad.

You are not alone. Your presence is valued. You will conquer the darkness. You just need to be patient with yourself and remember that what you feed your mind matters.

Anxiety and depression are very common, but we go through them in different ways. People look at me in awe when they hear my story. "But Kayla, you're so strong and outgoing." That's the point! I think there are a lot of people who are hiding their pain the same way I was, for whatever reason they may choose. I hope that this collection of poems might resonate with these ones, or at least continue to raise awareness.

Mental health is just as important as physical health.

depression / clinical
noun
1. a mental health disorder characterized by persistent feelings of severe despondency, dejection, and loss of interest, accompanied by an inability to carry out daily activities. *Mayo Clinic*

generalized anxiety disorder
noun
2. a medical mood disorder defined by excessive, persistent feelings of unprovoked dread, "even intrusive thoughts about certain fears or constant fear in general." *Monica Guirguis, DO*

happy poems

I wish I could write happy poems.

Why is it that my creativity thrives off of pain?
Why is my negativity the only thing I can explain?
Why are all the sad songs
the ones we're singing in the rain?
As if the rain itself isn't *already* enough to overflow the drains?

I wish I could.

I wish I could write happy poems.
I guess I finally realized
the truth between these lines;
The realest words sometimes hide
behind troubled minds.

So I find,
the truth we need might not be so cheerful,
but might actually be revealed
in what we once found fear for.

I wish I could write happy poems.
I really wish I could,
but if I would,

would it reach you?

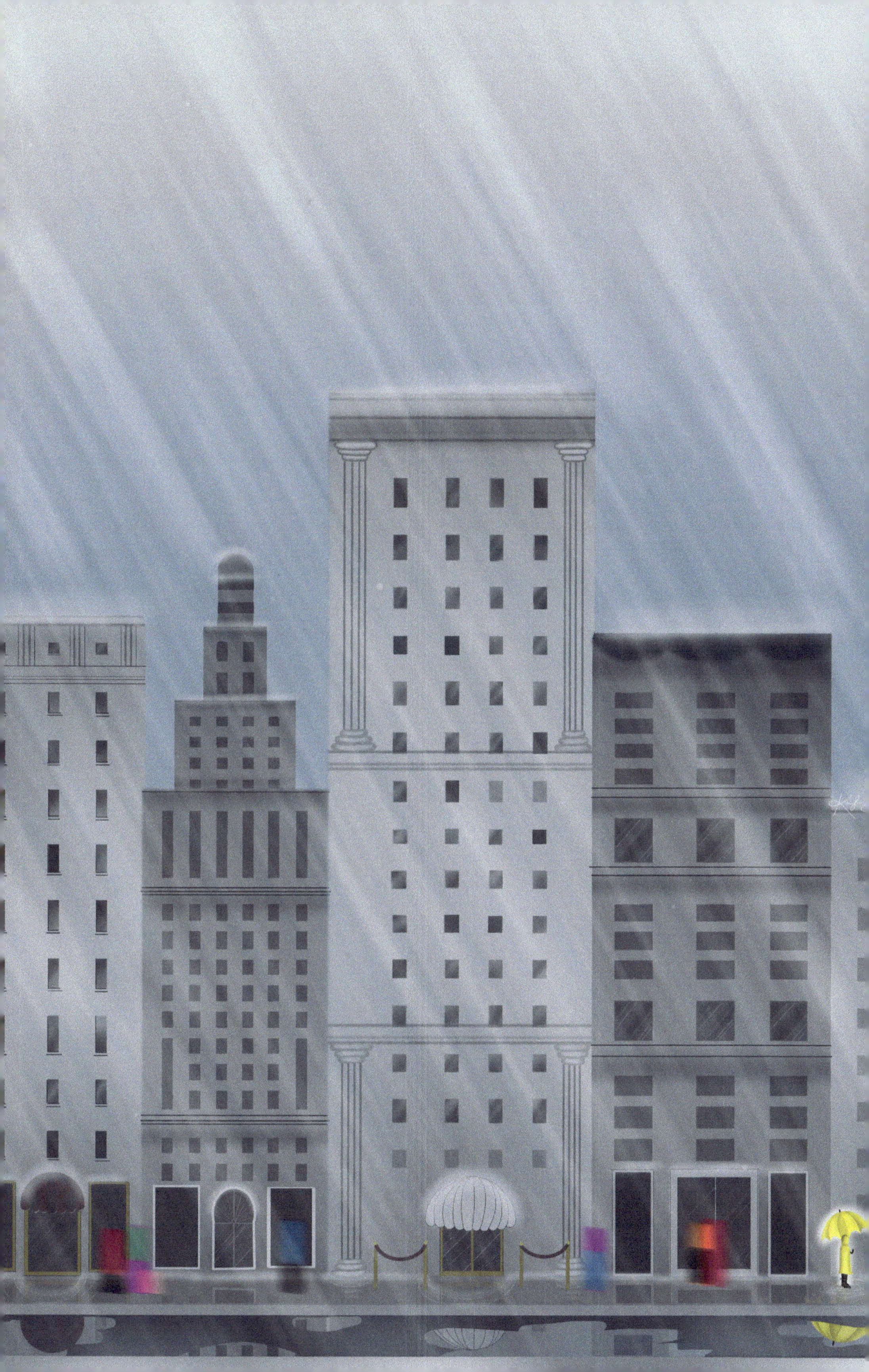

negative c h e m i s t r y

Even when they listen to my mind
somehow they still don't hear me.
I share with them my vision
and still they're not seeing it.
I share with them my story
but they have a hard time believing it.
I'm here.
With you,
and all of you are with me.
Somehow we are all here together, but my presence is still lacking.
I'm not really here, no,
I'm just an extra.
Just someone to fill the s p a c e until they're on to the
next one,

and even then, I still don't m a t t e r .

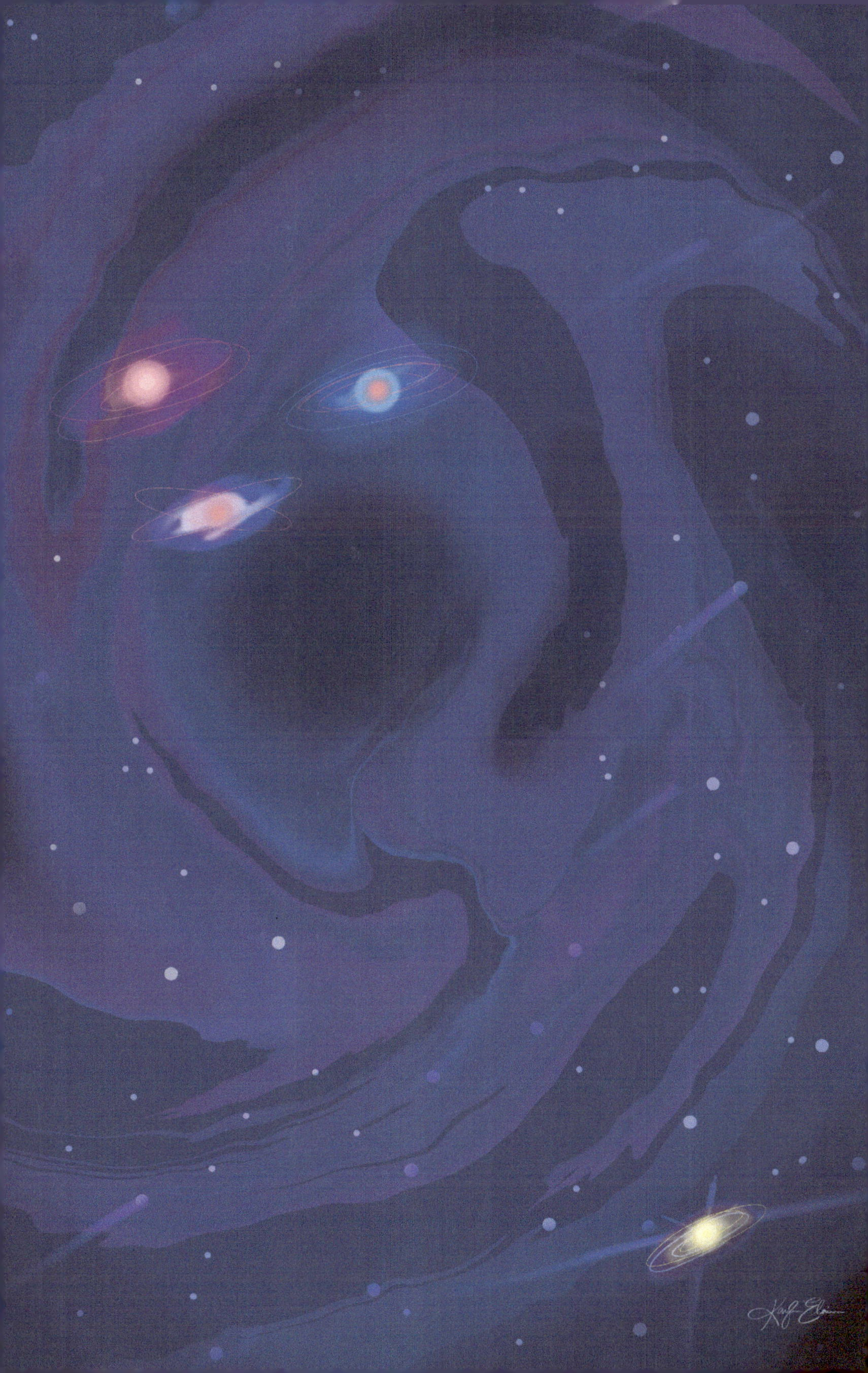

sometimes ...

Sometimes I feel like I'm falling apart,
like my favorite pieces keep drifting away.
I can see them—clear in front of me
but tragically, they're just beyond my reach.
Sometimes I just feel empty.
Not in my entirety,
but to have lost just enough of myself to notice.
Like out of the 80% I once was,
my glass is now half full.
I thought that adding you would increase its volume,
I thought adding you would fill my glass to its brim.
Sometimes I feel I'm broken.
Glass shattered, a pile full of pity.
Sometimes I try to put myself back together again
but what's the use when no one else can tell.
They don't see these cracks in my character.
They can't see the missing pieces.
My anguish is imperceptible,
my aching silence becoming lethal.
It's not your fault,
it's not mine either.
I am brilliant, I am beautiful,
I am scrappy, I am strong,
I am all of these things
and yet
I am none of them at all.

Sometimes.

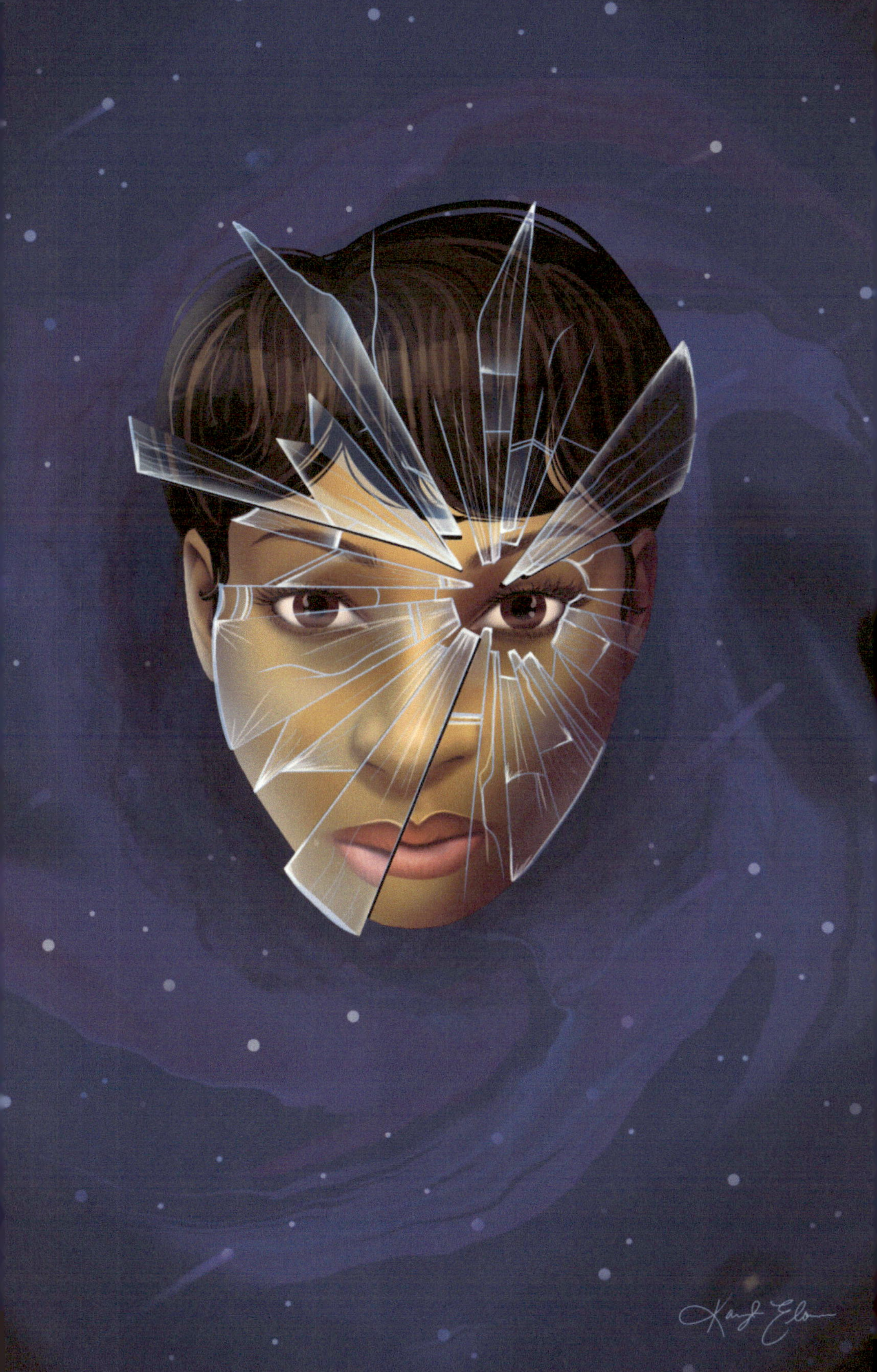

tnt: trials and tribulations

I wish I could take it back.
I regret everything.
Every word, every dig.
Everything that I did

that day.
Every mistake that I've made.
I lost my self-control and
watched my dignity detonate.

I'm ashamed of who I had
allowed myself to become.
All the pressure, all the trauma,
to all that anger I had succumbed.

I was tired of doing the right thing,
felt like I had nothing to show for it.
I was tired of holding my tongue.
I'm tired of always being the one—

The one whose love and support is unwavering.
Whose words of wisdom always prove to be strengthening.
The one who has it together, the one you can rely on.
Who has forgiven, more times than she herself could try on.

So, I combusted.
I guess my moral compass was rusted.
It must have gotten lost in these saltwater seas,
in the lack of better judgment in which I once trusted.

My whole morale, up in fumes.
I wasn't acting like myself,
I wasn't thinking things through.
Now I hope that you can forgive me

for exploding on you.

I'm sorry.

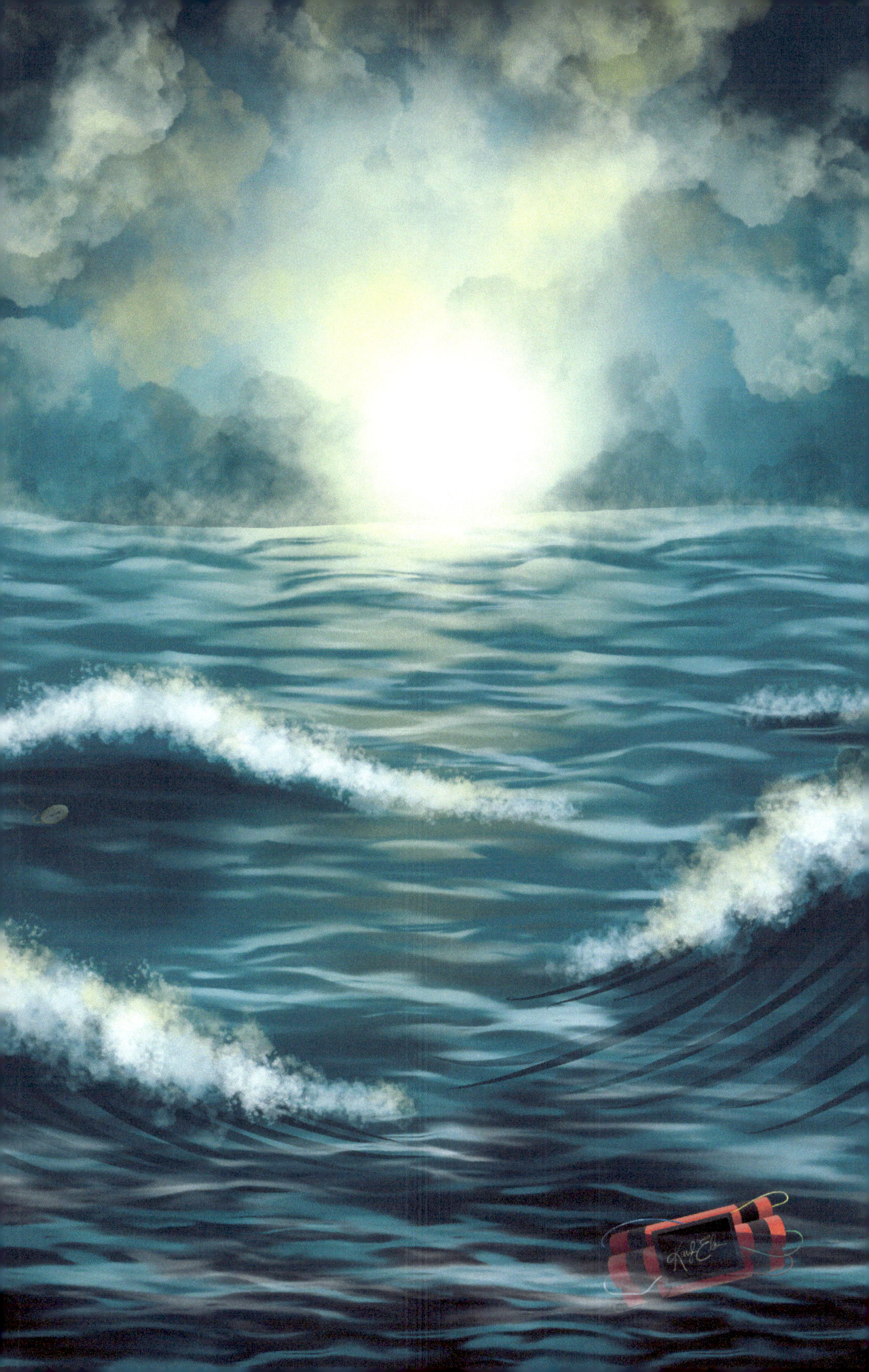

the blues

I hate myself.
I know that you must hate me too,

I think my favorite color might be yellow
just 'cause I hate feeling blue.

I hate the way the world makes it seem *so* easy
just to quit for something new.

Except I could never quit,
I'm not one to surrender.

That's why I'm always wrestling with my thoughts,
I'm my biggest contender.

A hopeless, waste of space in all my glory—
yes, futile in all my splendor.

Oh, to be normal.
But I'm a fraudster,
an imposter,
it's myself that I hinder.

My fists clench furiously.
My heart burns in anticipation.
My eyes sting in disappointment.
But there is no relieving it,

because the blundering blues
feeds on fake news,

and somehow I'm always believing it.

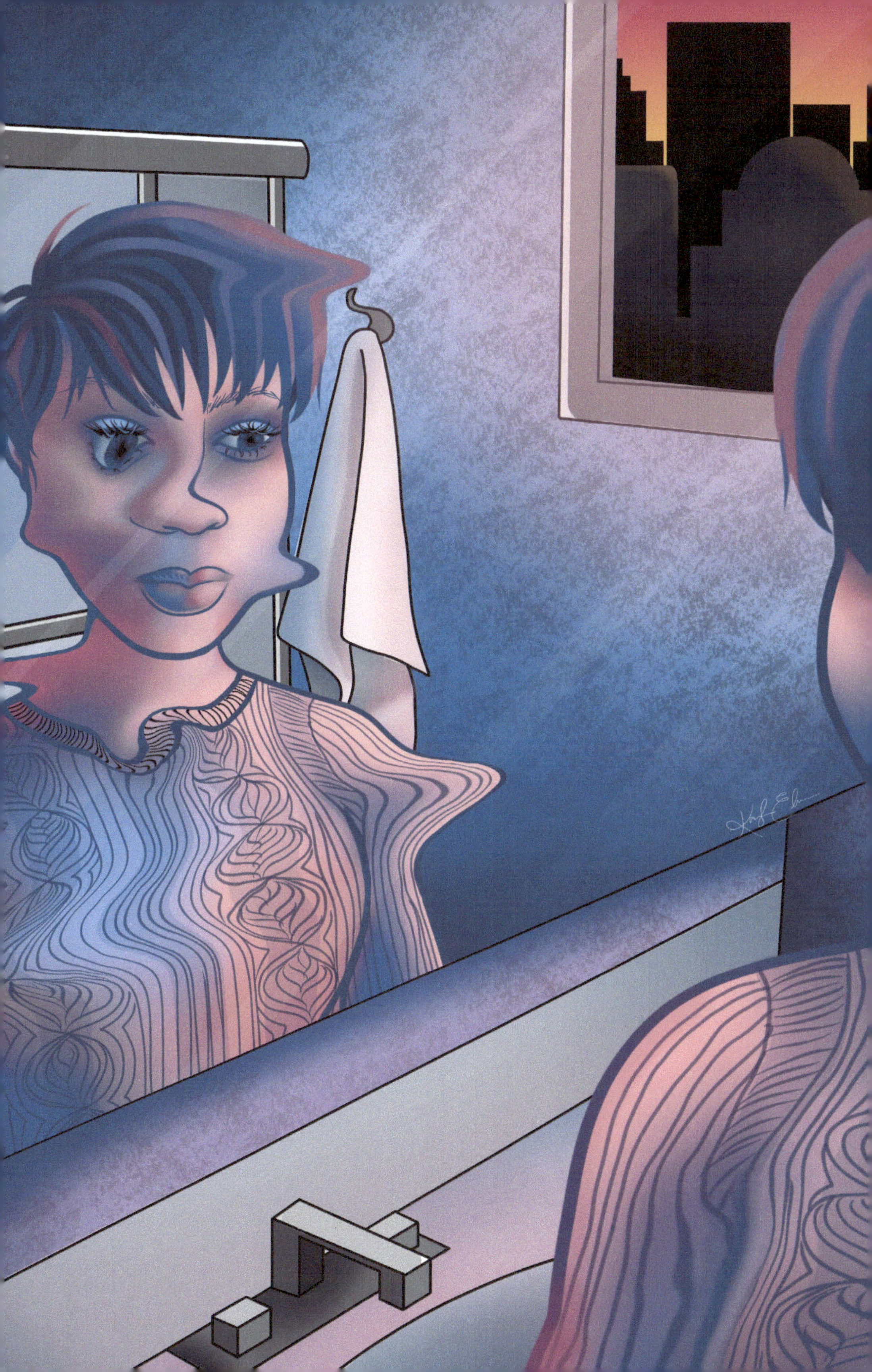

ataxia

All the lines in the room are, dancing?
Swaying and swinging.
I just stand still
and hear the chaos singing.

Out of focus,
all the colors begin to blur.
Now I can't focus,
and all of my thoughts begin to slur.

All the lines are dancing.
Switching and shifting.
Weightless in the head,
my acuity drifting.

Collapsing,
my heart drops to my gut.
Falling to the ground,
gravity's more than a construct.

I'm just stuck,
Suction-cupped to these vinyl tiles.
My worst fears flash within my mind
as if it's flipping through files.

Each breath that I take
gets quicker, thinner.
I should peel myself off the kitchen floor
because it's time to make dinner.

But   I   can't   move.

All the lines are *laughing*.
It's never my choice when I encounter these.
Not even my own mind
will respect my boundaries.

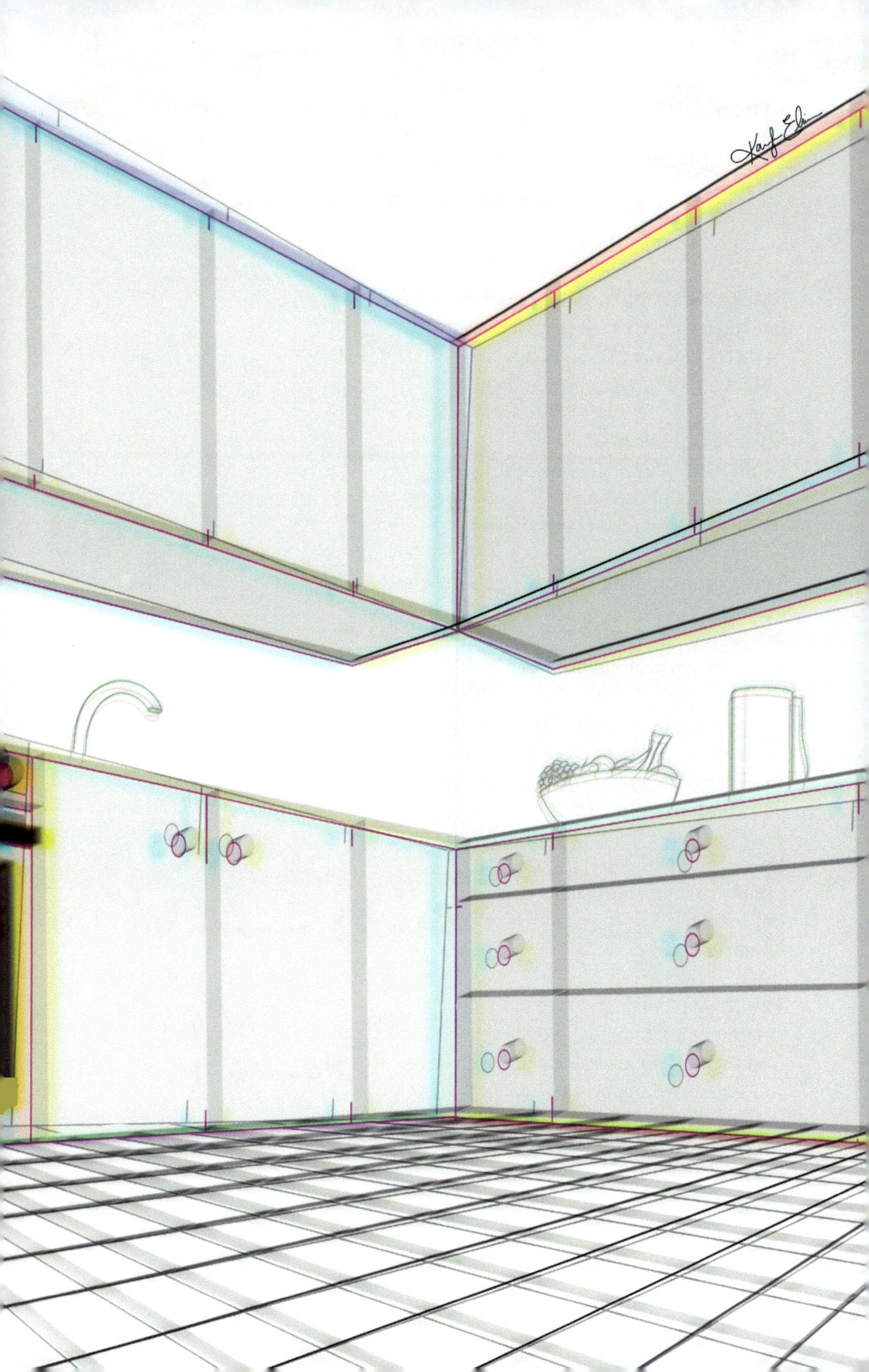

spinning

My heart is tattered.
My inner essence has been shattered,
I can't seem to stop reliving it
and it only makes me sadder.

Now I *wish* I could say that I feel empty
but the truth is, I feel quite the opposite.
In fact, I feel dizzy.
In fact, I feel too much.

My core temperature
could make a fever feel insignificant.
This feeling of confusion
in my mind seems to be infinite.

There is an agonizing gripping in my chest.
I can't —
inhale,
I can't even catch my breath.

There must be a knot-tying contest
using my vital organs as the rope,
as I try to wrap my mind around something
eons beyond my scope.

I wish it all was just a dream.
I know that you can't hear it,
but inside,
I just scream.

This, blood-curdling cry
ringing in my head will never cease.
And there is no justice for the murderous thoughts
robbing me of my peace.

I will never be the same.

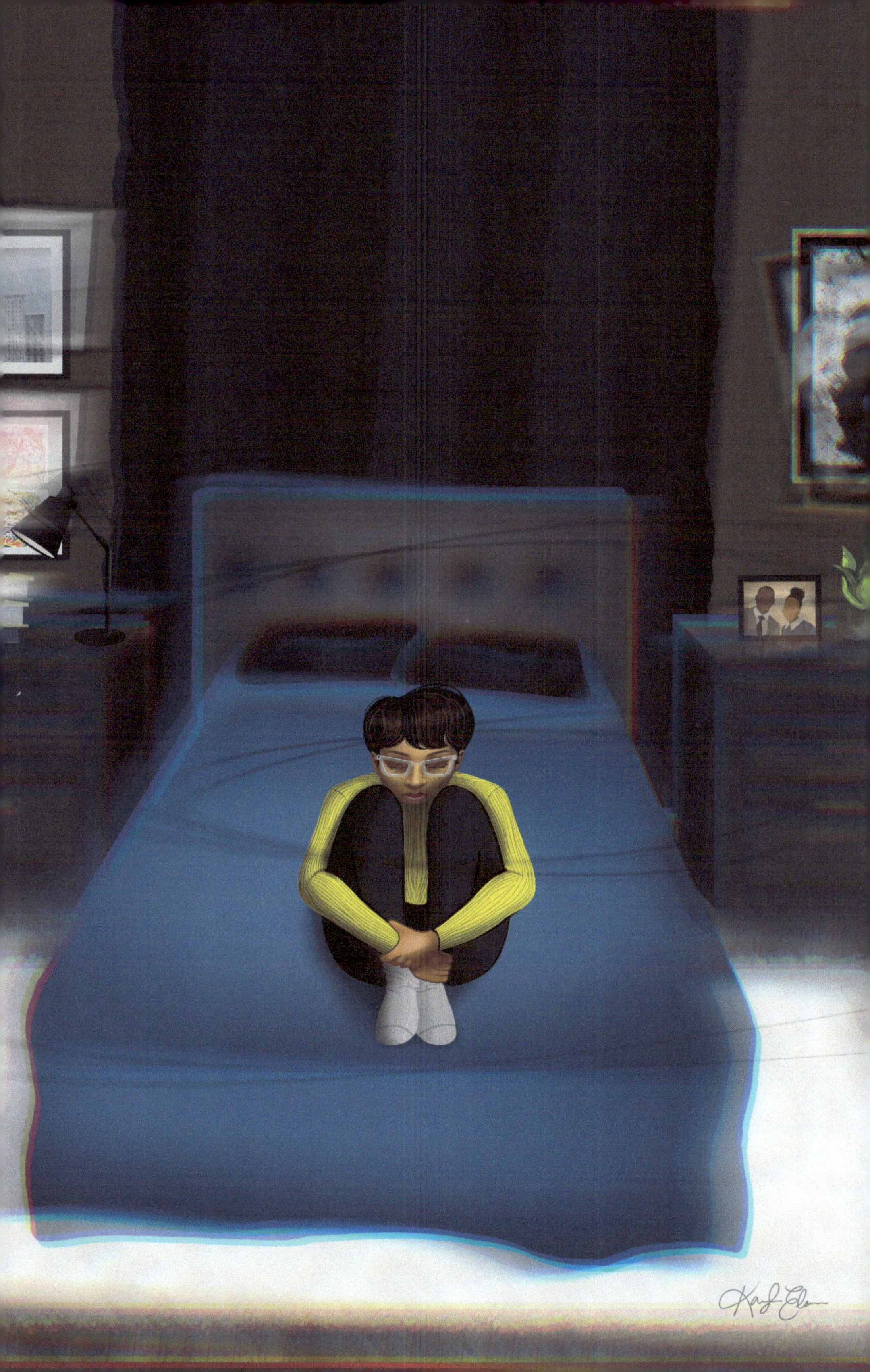

filled with loss

Time has left no space,
but only to retrace
all of the little moments that can never be replaced.
I haven't left the house in days
so now the mailbox is completely full.
I can't bear another text or call,
my *social* mailbox is completely full.
Days have dawned since I've last eaten,
yet somehow my stomach feels completely full.
I can't seem to think at all
but my mind still manages to be, completely full?

Today, my heart echoes completely hollow,
but the memory of you remains

completely full.

every mourning ,

Every morning ,
I resurrect
and wash the blood off my bones.
I clothe myself in happy skin,
and then, away I go.
I have to smile and I have to wave.
Here and there I might throw in a nod.
I've got this, "super-glued composure,"
so that I don't break this façade.
Then, at the end of the day,
I return to my grave.
Only to find
a desperate glimpse of hope
trying to brighten my cave.
Okay, wait.
The hope starts to glimmer...
My bones start to shimmer...
The grief starts to ease,
and my troubled heart seems so pleased.
But eventually, the hope has to leave...

and my heart has to bleed.

Until I die again,
and the cycle repeats.

Every morning ,

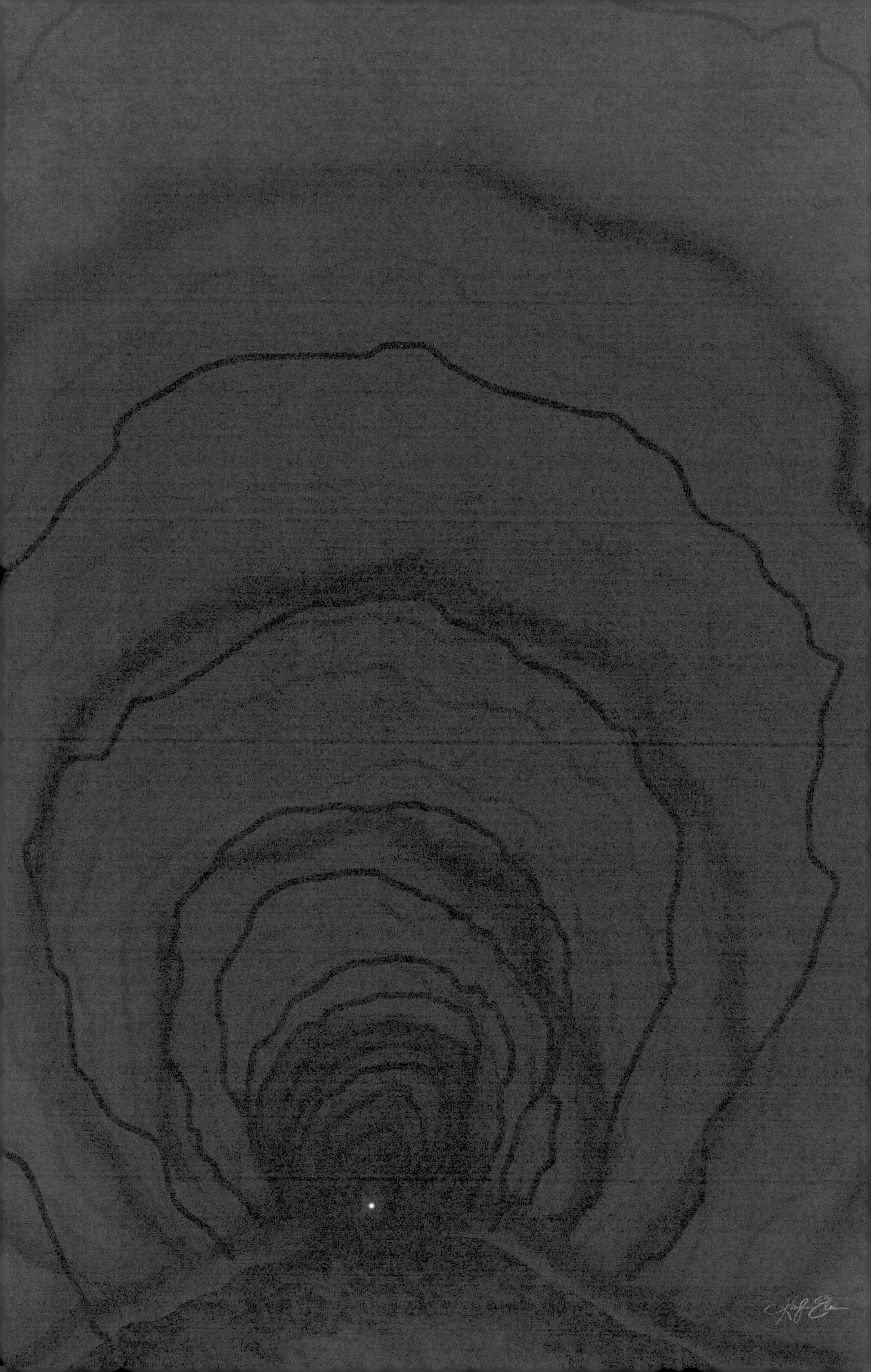

just breathe

Last time wasn't so bad.
I guess it could have been a lot worse.

"Wait, are you serious?"

Did I forget to put my wallet in my purse?
You know what, I don't have time for this today.
Nope, go back, because today would be the day.
I'd be pulled over with no ID before I even hit the highway.
Okay, okay, forget it.
Back up the stairs again.
Girl, you may be thin but you are out of shape, my friend.
If I didn't feel so hopeless maybe I'd go to the gym—
Oh, there's my wallet,
I guess I dropped it on the floor.
Oh—there's that one thing I was looking for.
Where's the other—
I have to get back in the car.
ETA 15 minutes

"Did I lock the door?"

And of course.
Great, there's a detour.
Another 10 minutes.
This is why you get up early! Why can't I just get up early?
If I could get a full night's rest but that almost happens rarely.
Uh-uhn. No. What was that noise?
That sounded expensive.
At this point, this car's repairs would definitely be extensive.
I am   so   tired.
I'm exhausted, I'm expended.

"I SWEAR THIS ETA HAS **ONE MORE TIME**
TO BE EXTENDED."

I can barely keep up with medical bills,
not to mention the money *already* spent on "all-weather" wheels.
Maybe the noise is nothing,
Maybe my car is bluffing,
Maybe I'll just pretend that I don't hear all that muffling.
But—
What if the engine fails and I die in a crash?
What if it just explodes and I blow up in ash?
I mean, would that be so bad?
Now my heart is pounding, am I really that sad?
What is wrong with me?

I feel like I'm on edge,
I can't seem to pull it together
to talk myself down from the ledge.

"Let Me Merge!"

Maybe I need to stretch?
Maybe I'm just too stressed.
I still haven't checked on So-and-So,
despite my sincerest pledge.
What kind of friend am I?
Why do I even try?
Why do I get my hopes up just to fail every time?
I bet they think I'm careless.
They probably couldn't care less.

"I can't show up like this."

I'm a wreck, I'm a mess.
Yeah. Now I'm not in the mood at all.
It's way too late to cancel, I couldn't dare to make that call.
Should I even go to this?
I shouldn't even go.
They probably wouldn't notice,
I'll just—
No.
I just need to pull over,
now I'm feeling like I can't breathe.
I hope nobody's watching me, as I let out a sharp scream.

"DID I EVEN LOCK THE DOOR?"

I guess since I'm almost there, I might as well go.
I'll dry my face with this Chipotle napkin; they won't even know.

Just b r e a t h e.

w h h h h h h w

"Hey! Oh my goodness, it's so good to see you."

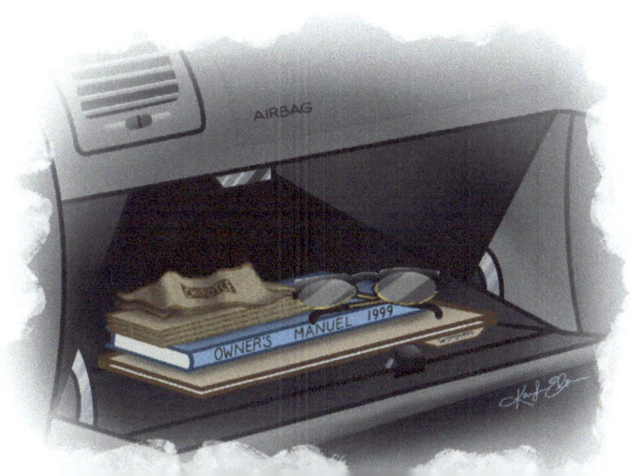

i'm good

What happened to the girl who was stronger than this?
What happened to her drive and her confidence?
This isn't you.
Come on now, get it together.

I've always hated the wintertime; it must be the weather.
Yeah, this is that, "seasonal depression."
I'll be back to myself by mid-March, without question.
I'll be, back and better once I pack up these sweaters.

I was tripping.
I mean for real, I am *not* that sad.
I don't even know why I'm crying, life is *not* that bad.
This, unidentified loom of gloom is only making me mad.

** Tchhp **

I'm good.

(1 Corinthians 10:12) *NWT*

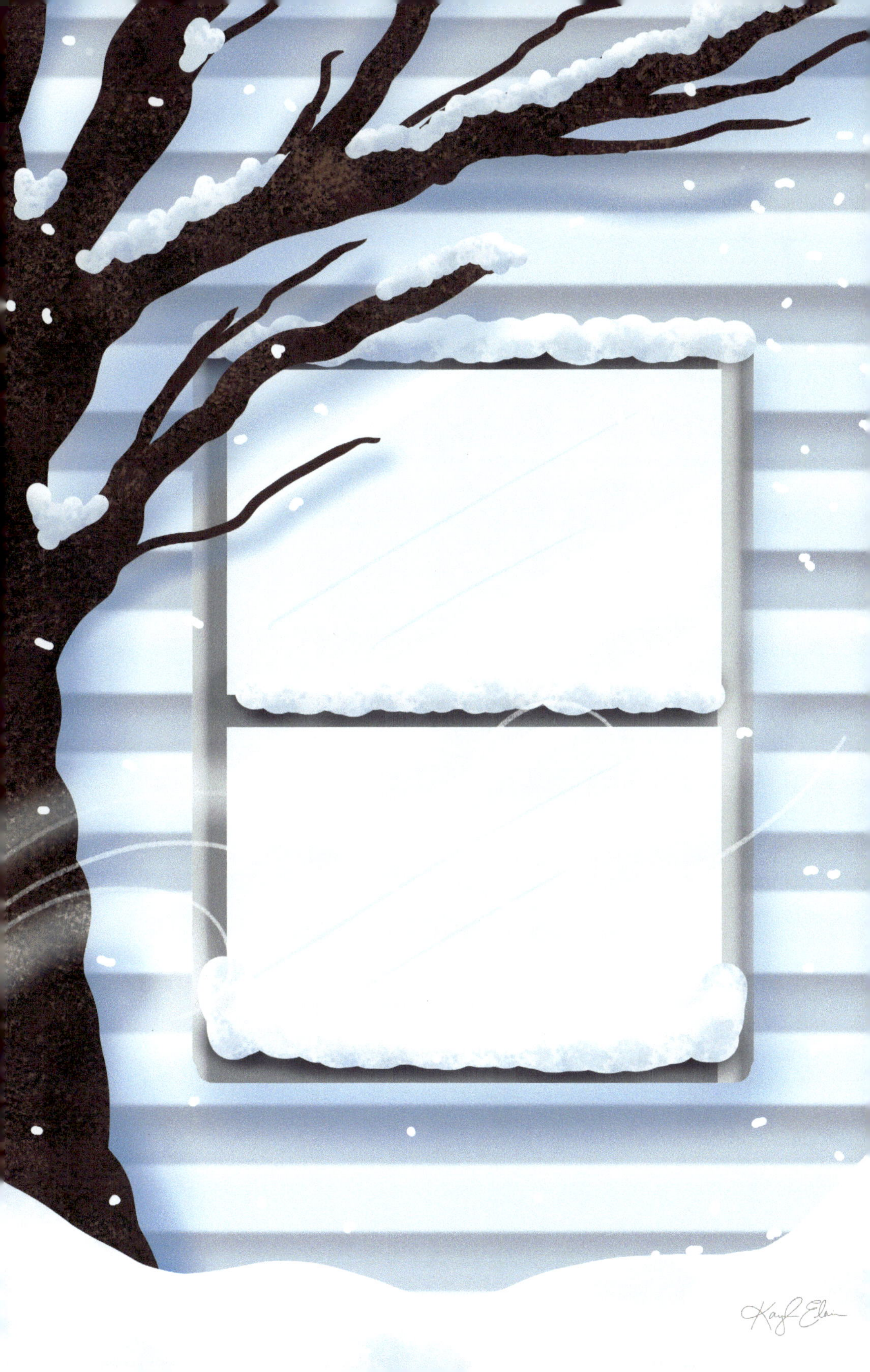

mutiny of the mind

Why do I feel this way?
Life may not be perfect, but like overall I'm okay?
Yet, my mind is racing ever more rapidly by the day.
I can't sit still,
I can't even *begin* to describe how I feel.
I don't recognize my own intentions, and the feeling's surreal.

You crept into my mind without asking permission.
At first, I didn't even notice.
I had no suspicion.
Like a predator to prey, you saw my heart's condition.
I felt weakened and betrayed
so you took your position.
Doused me with tear gas, now I'm out of commission.
Clouded my judgment, now I see things through foggy vision.
Disoriented, I felt so alone.
You set out to wage war
on my mind's once happy home.
Now faced with the unknown,
it's safe to say I've entered an uncharted war-zone.
I was not equipped,
I had no idea what to expect, and
absolutely *nothing* could have prepared me for what would happen next.

One by one
you captured pieces of my character.
Stripped me of my confidence,
left me lifeless like a caricature.
Enslaved my emotions,
imprisoned my inspiration,
cut off my creativity
and replaced it with isolation.
Humiliated my "happiness,"
decapitated my dignity,
annihilated my aspirations
and sapped me of my energy.

Until there was nothing left.
I tried to run; down to my very last breath.
Then you turned me against myself
so I could finish the rest.

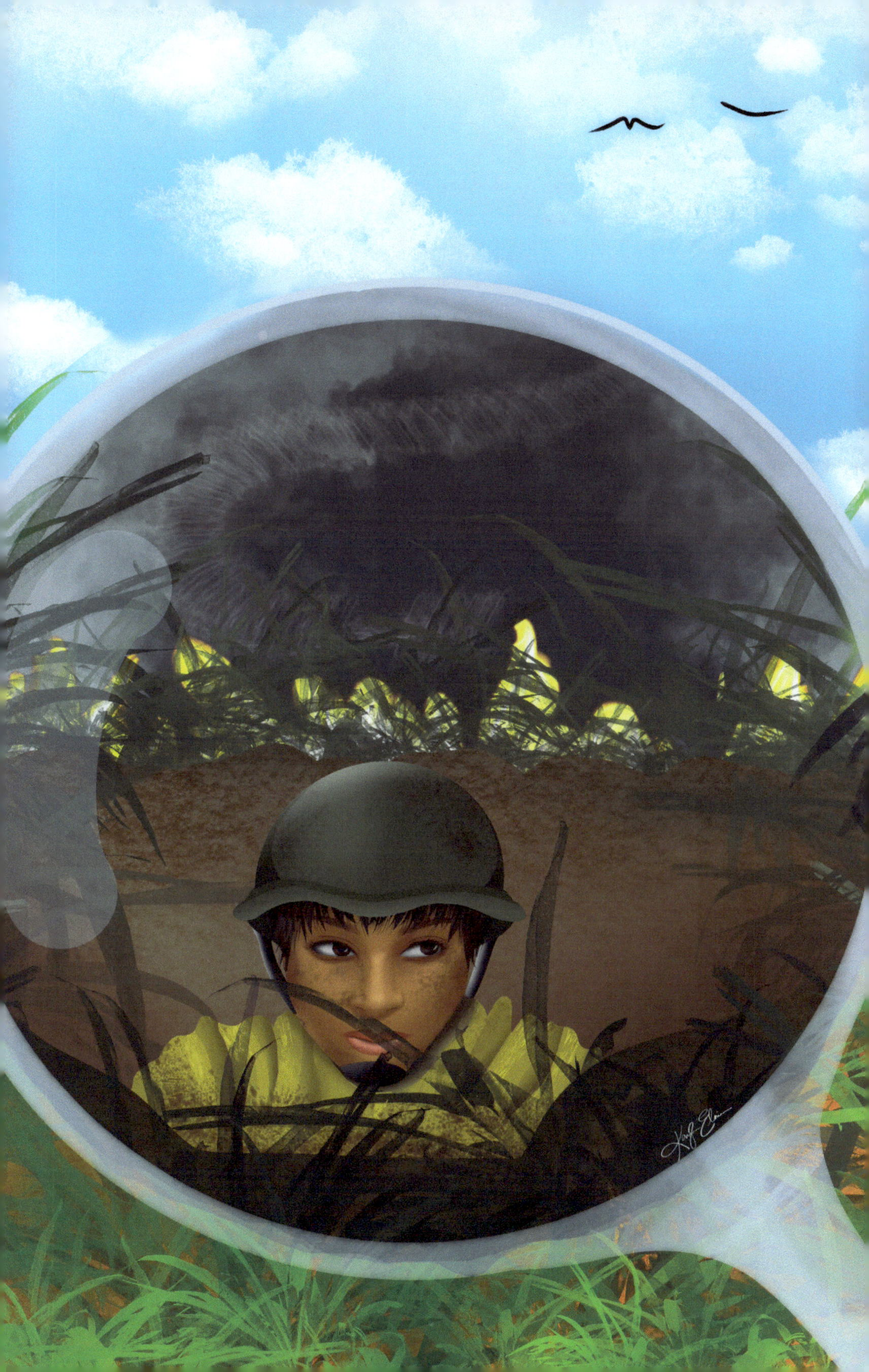

black hole

How do you drown in a sea that no one else sees?
Quietly, ignoring the urge to scream. And
how do you fill a broken glass?
Exhaustingly, in hopes that one day it just might last.

How do you see through bloodshot eyes?
Quite easily, to my surprise.
I want to cry out for help, but I just can't seem to get it out.
With all my might, but quite inaudibly, I shout.

Can you hear it in my happy voice?
Do you see it in my smiling eyes?
Encrypted in my cheerful spirit is the truth of my demise.

Tears suppressed through what appears to be a stream of
endless heartaches.
I can manage a broken bone, but what do you do when your
soul breaks?

Can you become whole again?
Or do you just fall victim to that hole again?
Over and over.
Tripping on the rotten roots that have now blossomed into a trend.

A black hole,
wit-fully drawing you in.
Tirelessly fighting evil thoughts so that you might rise again.

And you will.
Because you always do.
The sad cycle of emotional warfare is tough.

But it's not tougher than you.

You have faith.

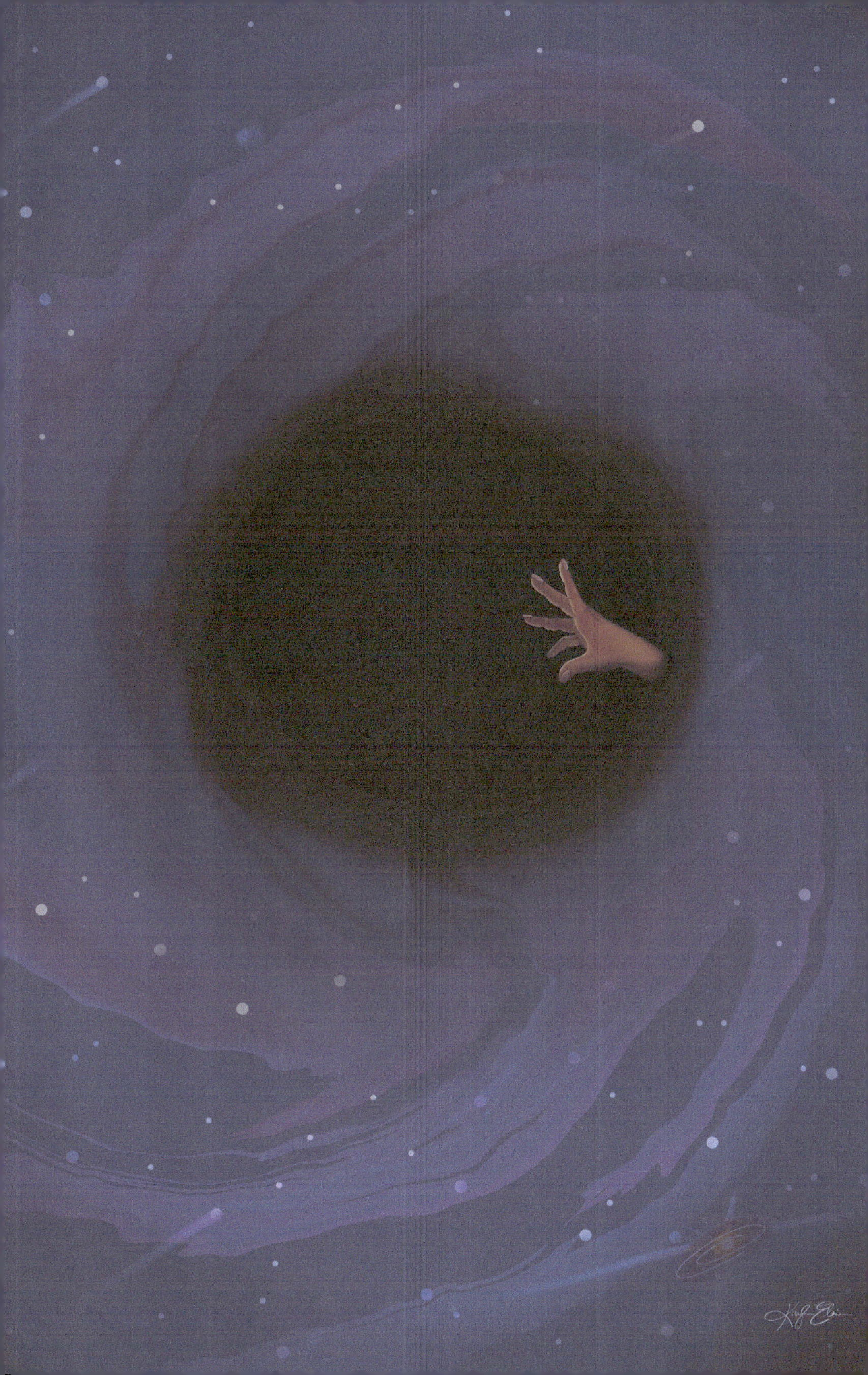

catch me before i fall

Pay attention, you don't see me slipping away?
You don't seem to get it, there's nothing left for me to say.
I feel like I'm losing it. No, I don't need to go to therapy.
I'm not asking for too much, I just need you to be there for me.

This is a vicious cycle.
And I can't seem to break free
from these fictitious shackles
enslaving me.

Clenched fists, engrave fingernail tips into sweaty palms.
I am taunted by my own inner anarchist.
I am haunted by a longing to no longer exist.
Should I see a therapist?

I can see it now.
Do you *see* that silence?
I can feel it now.
Can you *feel* that darkness?

No. This is not the end,
I have so much more to live for.
I'm only 24, I'm sure
there's so much more in store.

There has to be.
Do I have the courage to find out?
Am I willing to be vulnerable?
Is my faith stronger than my doubt?

I need to get out of here,
but I don't trust myself to drive.
There's just way too much hurt
impairing my will to stay alive.

I don't think I can do this.
Is it fear, is it pride?
Now I'm being foolish.
If I don't, I won't survive.

I need therapy. (Psalm 55:2) *NWT*

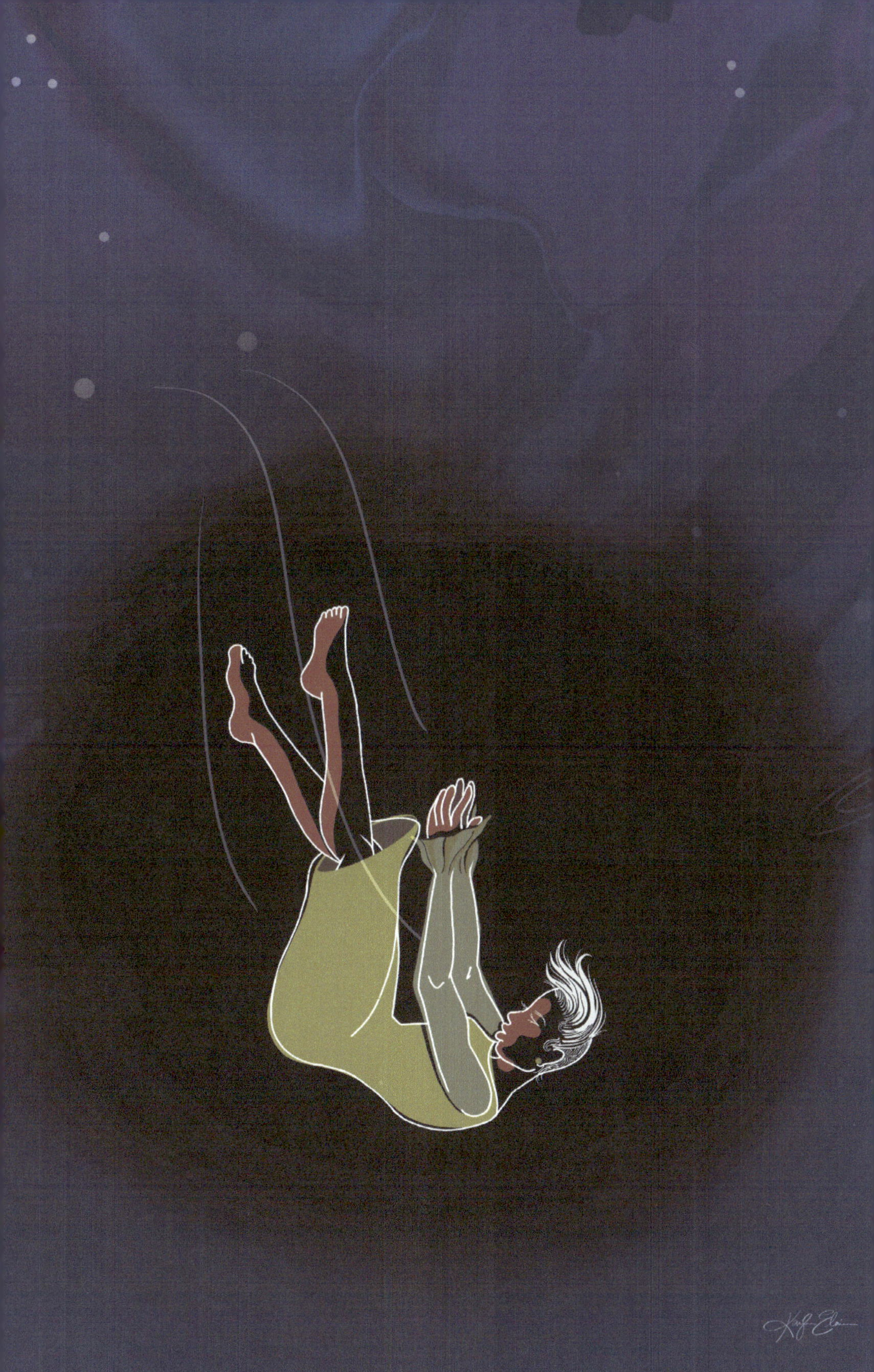

hues

Desperate and confused,
I threw my anxiety on Him in a confessional
and He gave me the courage
to seek the help of a professional.

Unsure of the possibilities,
I had no choice but to, clothe myself in humility.
I had to, acquire new tools
to nurse my mind to rehability.

Mrs. PHD, thank you for enlightening me.
Unraveling before my very eyes
was the life I thought I always knew
and now I can see why:

I can see why I was stuck,
why I was so confused.
I can see when it all began,
when that yellow changed hues.

A little dimmer
for all the verbal abuse that I chose to excuse.
A little darker
every time my self-esteem took a bruise.

Even duller.
Self-destructive behavior, my new muse.
A change in color.
No more of that hopeful spirit they were so used to.

I see how suppressing emotions
censored my right to feel,
how that nagging commitment to my image
hindered my right to heal.

In pursuit of regaining mental stability,
I first had to accept myself, in all of my fragility.
All that rattling within, always battling against
the justification for my pain and its validity.

Red flags were flying, but each one I kept denying.
Alarms were going off, but I must've hit the snooze.
Way back then, I couldn't see the clues.
But now that I have learned that I can choose...

I choose to heal.

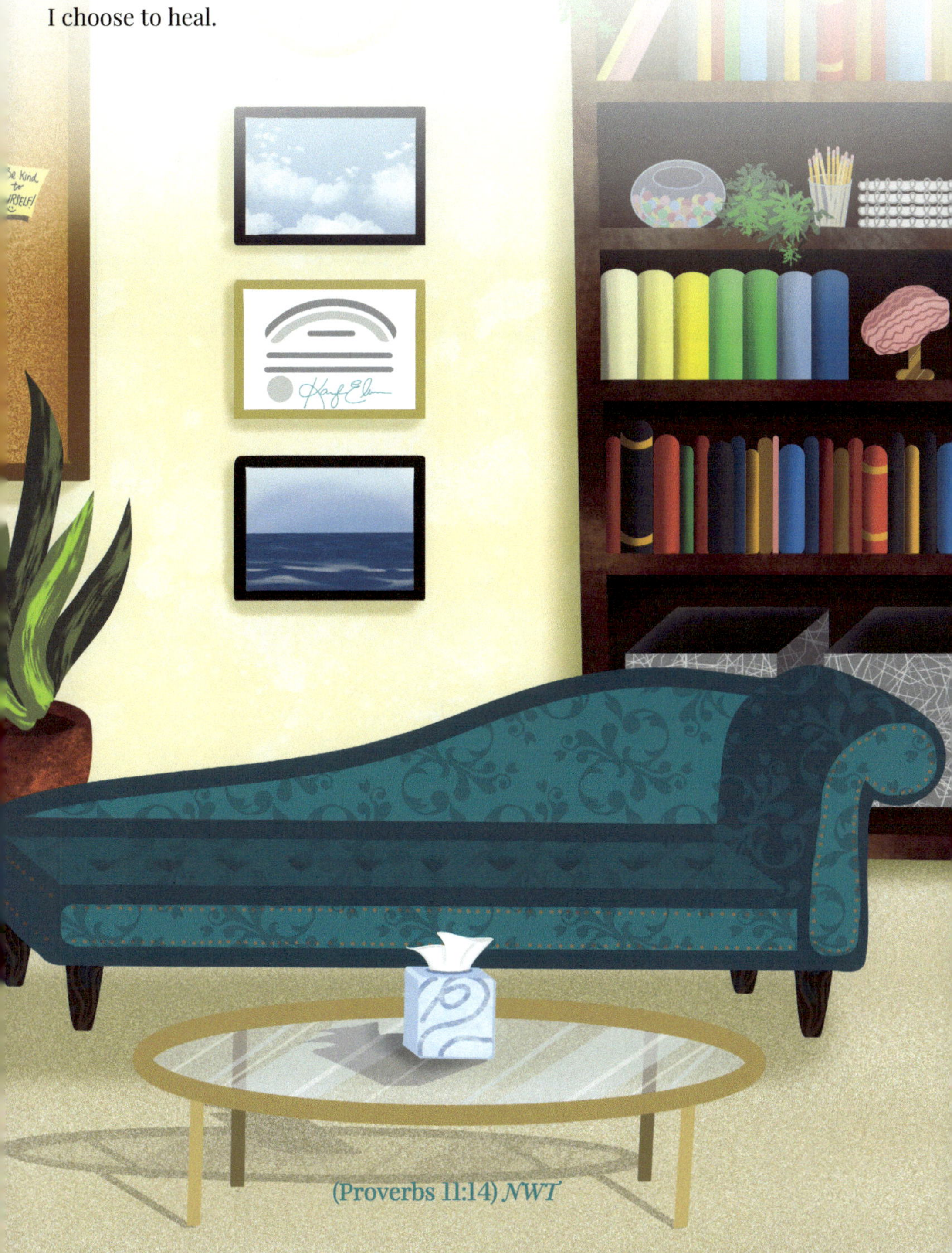

(Proverbs 11:14) *NWT*

shaped by the lies I was told

I was told, little girls "like me"
weren't *worth* much.
So, you see, I couldn't *afford* to be so sensitive,
I had to be tough.
I was told I had to be smarter
and "work 10 times harder" than everyone else to succeed.
Because I entered into this little game called life, with the
mode "already set on the hardest difficulty."
I was just a little girl back then.

I thought that, making straight A's and playing the violin
could make up for the color of my skin.
I thought excelling in every subject
would drown the doubts I felt deep within.
But it's only *the secret person of the heart*
that truly matters in the end.
I was lead to believe that "my value depended
only upon what I could give or provide."
But it was that very lack of setting boundaries for myself
that left me with no choice but to hide.

It was either, "black girl magic,"
or I was just black girl tragic.
There was no in between.
Either I was a slave, or a queen.
Either way it went, there was no room for me
to just be me. Either way,
I was forced to disprove or to choose
to live up to these, augmented realities.
I had been convinced that the mistreatment I endured
would only "make me stronger."
Each and every wronger
couldn't have been any wronger.
I was torn down.

Yet and still, my glimmering crown held accolades.
It alone stood tall. Stacking each accomplishment high,
shined, and polished with each compliment of praise.
I worked hard, to be this good at hiding behind my talents.
But where can you hide within your own mind?
See now, *that* became the challenge.

I had been spoon-fed *so* many lies within my formative years.
Each opinion would become ammunition.
I'd answer the opposition with ambition,
so as not to form any tears.

Lying awake at night, paralyzed by my fears.
Fears of never being good enough.
I stand before you today,
the product of a misconception centuries old.

I was shaped—by the lies I was told.

my mother's shoes

We didn't always see eye to eye,
my mother and I.
I had to, "stay in a child's place."
I had no right to speak my piece.
I had no right to let off steam.
I had no method of release,
I was just
pressure cooked.
My feelings were often overlooked.
For all the arguments we had,
we'd have enough to write a book.

But, you always had the best of intentions,
despite the dissonance, and the emotional distance.
You did your best with what you were given,
and gave the best of what you had.
You could only pour out but so much
because who was there, pouring into you?
When I see things from your point of view
I realize, I couldn't walk a mile in your shoes.

Who was there, teaching you to be soft
when you had your siblings and cousins to raise?
Who was holding *your* hand?
Telling *you* everything would be okay?
Who was in your corner cheering you on,
giving you praise?
Who was your listening ear on those
unrelenting days?

You didn't have a gentle mother's hug
to sweeten the bitter taste of reality.
She wasn't equipped to nurture you
and neither was *her* mother undoubtedly.
Ironclad,
stone-cold women from generations past,
passing it on to the next, no questions asked.
Fire tested, proven to withstand the heat.
But who wants to hug an open flame,
and who's to blame for this conceit?

You rarely said, I love you.
No, instead you said,
"Dinner is ready."
"Baby, that girl is *not* your friend."
"Did you pray about it?"
"Don't overreact, time always tells."
Though your **words** *whispered* "I love you,"
your **actions** *shouted* from the depths of the well.

You modeled the kind of loyalty that makes me a better friend.
You taught me the kind of beauty that only starts from within.
You taught me the kind of love that triumphs over sin.
You gave me the kind of wisdom it took you years to hone in.

I was too soft, too sensitive, wearing my heart on my sleeve.
You knew the world would chew me up and spit me out;
You were worried about me.

You've walked a million miles and back
in those carpenter boots.
Calloused to the jabs that the world would throw at you.
All you truly wanted was for **me**,
to be "invincible" too.

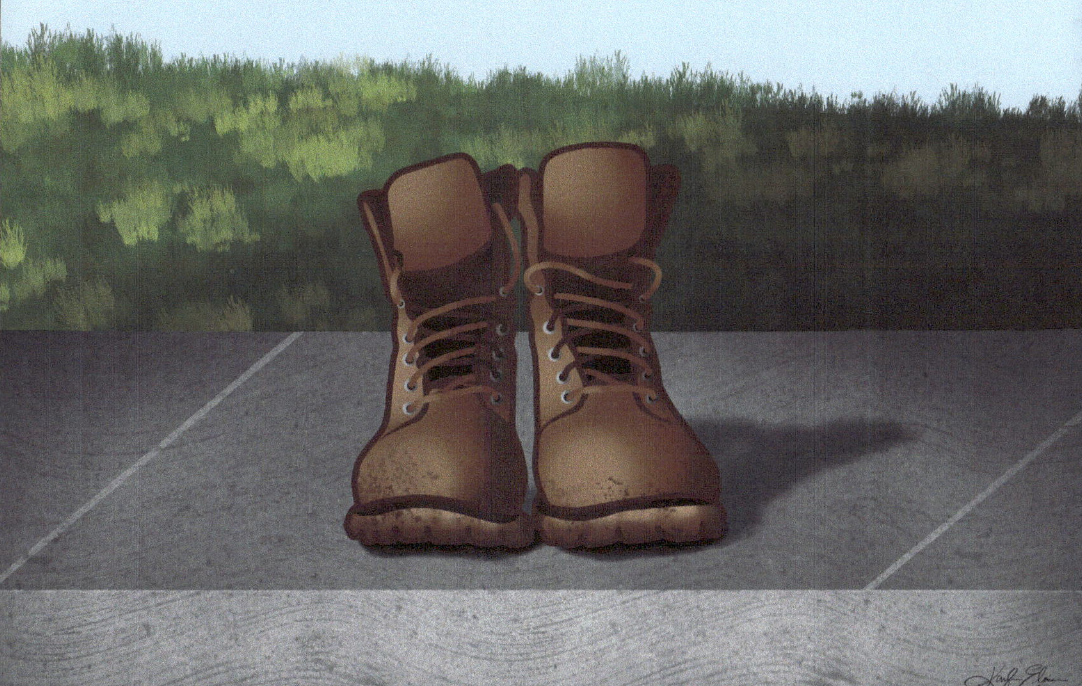

my dearest king,

To me, you were everything.
I had a sort of, *divine reverence*
for your presence, thing.
But I was young, and unalarmed by
the hypocrisy embedded in your essence.
Still, my young heart cleared space for you,
the epitome of acquiescence.
In my heart, you were untouchable
incorruptible, indestructible.
In my heart, you were a king on a throne,
up on a pedestal.

I didn't know that you were gone so long
'cause you were locked up in a cell.
I didn't know that having you back
would make Mommy yell.
I didn't know that when you left at night
you'd drink until you fell.
And I didn't know that I was the only one
believing the lies you'd tell.
    "Daddy's just a little silly right now."
    "Daddy loves Mommy so much."
    "Daddy won't ever hurt you."
    "Daddy will never leave."
Well I am not that little girl anymore,
much less am I naive.
I am a strong, God-fearing woman now.
Not one so easily deceived.

Where were *you*, when we had no heat?
When Mom was scraping pennies together
so we could have something to eat?
You weren't there.
Instead, you waged war with my faith.
I needed a father not a pastor, I felt so betrayed.

You left your kingdom collapsing,
clinging to your pious opinions so inertly.
That's why my heart stands fortified behind this Watchtower,
no gate left open for you to hurt me.

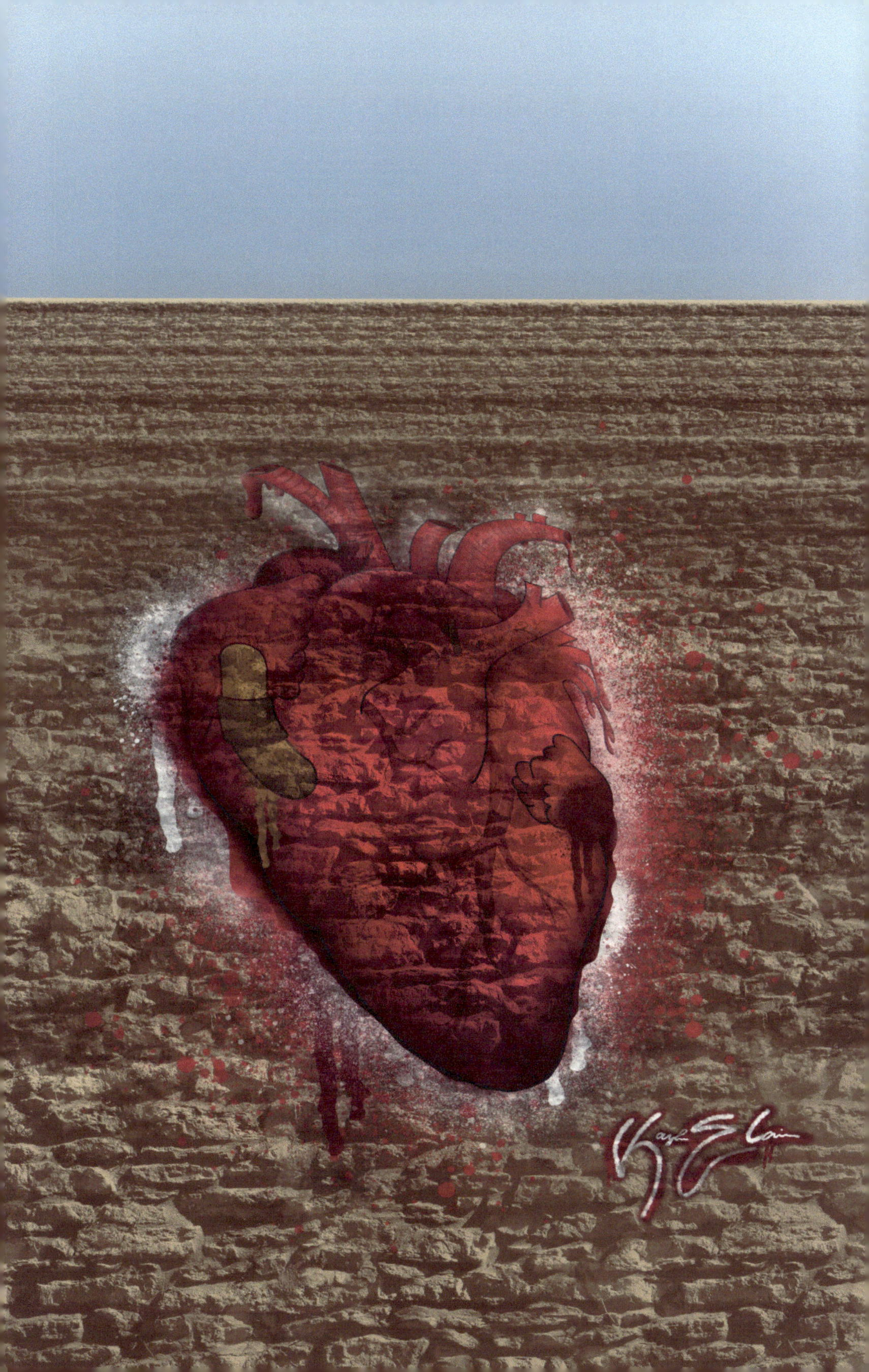

“don't cry over spilled milk”

It's those late nights.
The 1's, 2's & 3's
that have me deep into my thoughts,
like, myself is getting to know me.
Wrapped up, in this type of emotion
that holds true to them all.
I experience this emotion
frequently in the winter and fall.
Indescribably undesirable,
Unreliable, but undeniable.

I'm in my feelings.

Mad at the world and what it's come to.
Proud of my past
though, the future's the one I run to.
Hoping for a better day.
Grateful for those better days.
Forgiven the spilled milk but never forgotten,
it always stays.

It's like it's stained,
but like, the tablecloth is white?
Because, although you could never see it,
it’s still there.
And I know that it’s still there.
So I still care.
I still try
to wipe away the dried remains of that old stain
but the crust just crumbles
and I still cry.

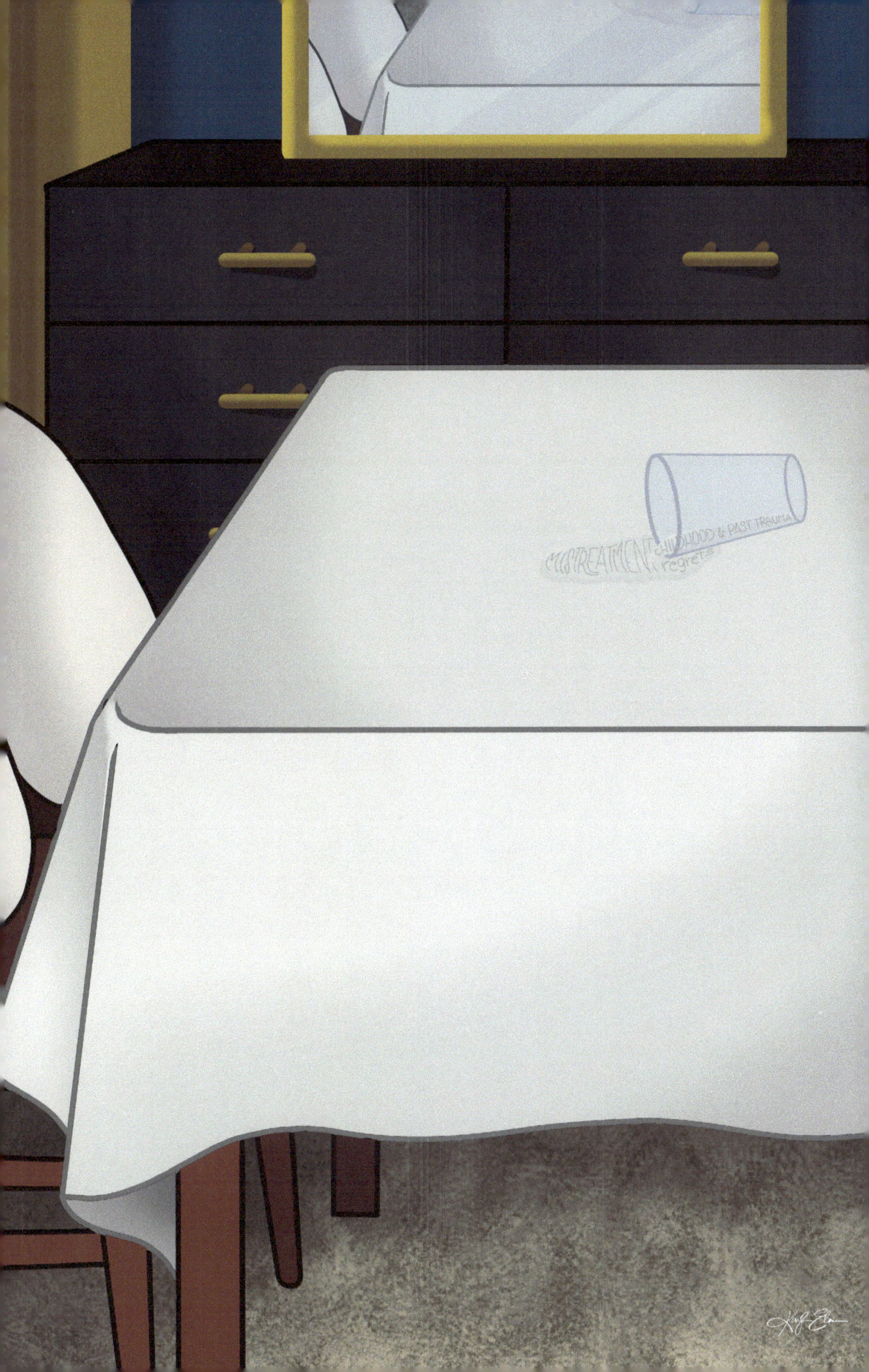
MISTREATMENT
CHILDHOOD & PAST TRAUMA
regrets

she cries

Once upon a time,
there lived
a little girl who wasn't *allowed*
to cry.

Now,
that *grown* woman
cries
all the time.

Good for her.

(Psalm 56:8)

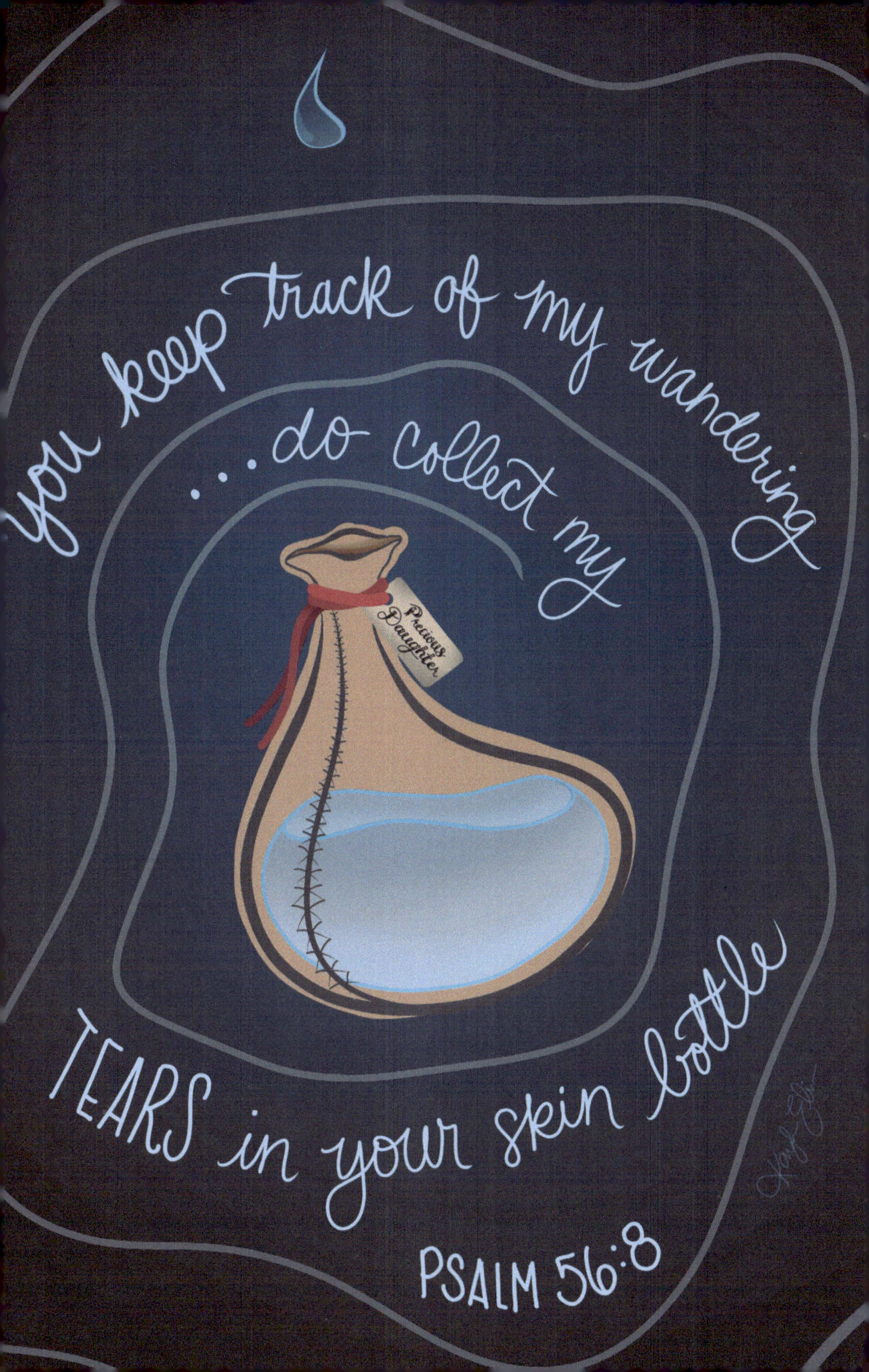

you keep track of my wandering

...do collect my

Precious Daughter

TEARS in your skin bottle

PSALM 56:8

hydrate daily

The wind rips
through my cracked lips.
Gasping for air, I can't breathe.
I'm dehydrated.

Eyelids scratchy like sandpaper
weighed down and weary.
The sun, beating with fury,
I'm exhausted from the heat.

I fell out of routine.
My head is pounding,
the ringing is resounding.
I'm feeling faint.

It's been days since
I truly *absorbed* your Word.
I can't seem to concentrate
and my vision is blurred.

Days turn to weeks,
now I'm in this desert all alone.
I won't make it on my own
I pray you don't desert me.

The wind rips
through my cracked lips.
Gasping for air, I can't breathe.
I'm dehydrated.

In the distance I see a mirage.
She calls out to me,
"Take life's water free,
your flesh is weak, hydrate daily."

I gaze into her
through the glass of a mirror,
and I peer into the Bible
to help me see her clearer.

(Romans 15:4, Revelation 22:17) *NWT*

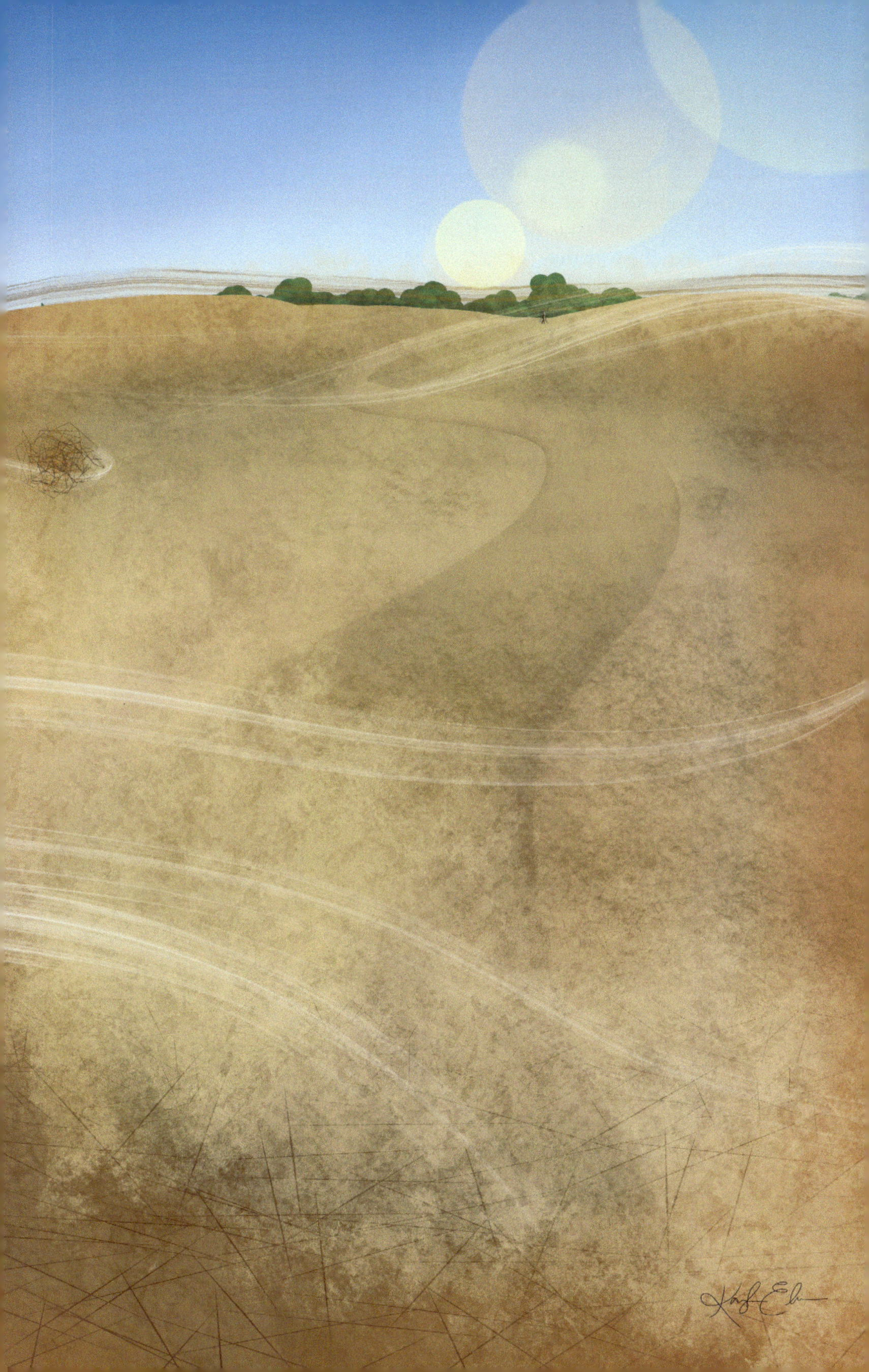

as far as it depends on me

I can't change the past
and I have no control over what lies ahead.
But I *can* control my actions
and what happens inside my own head.
I *can* change the way that I think.
No one is responsible for my own happiness
but me. So,
As far as it depends upon me
I will choose peace.
Peace first within myself.
I choose to make peace with the chaos.
To water my own garden
of love, of faith, prosperity.
Then I choose to forgive
whatever ripple affecting the stream of my emotional being.
And I choose to foster a secure environment
for the ones around me,
a safe haven
for those that I love.
A tranquil river,
refreshing whoever happens to cross my path.
Only I,
am responsible
for me.

(Romans 12:18) *NWT*

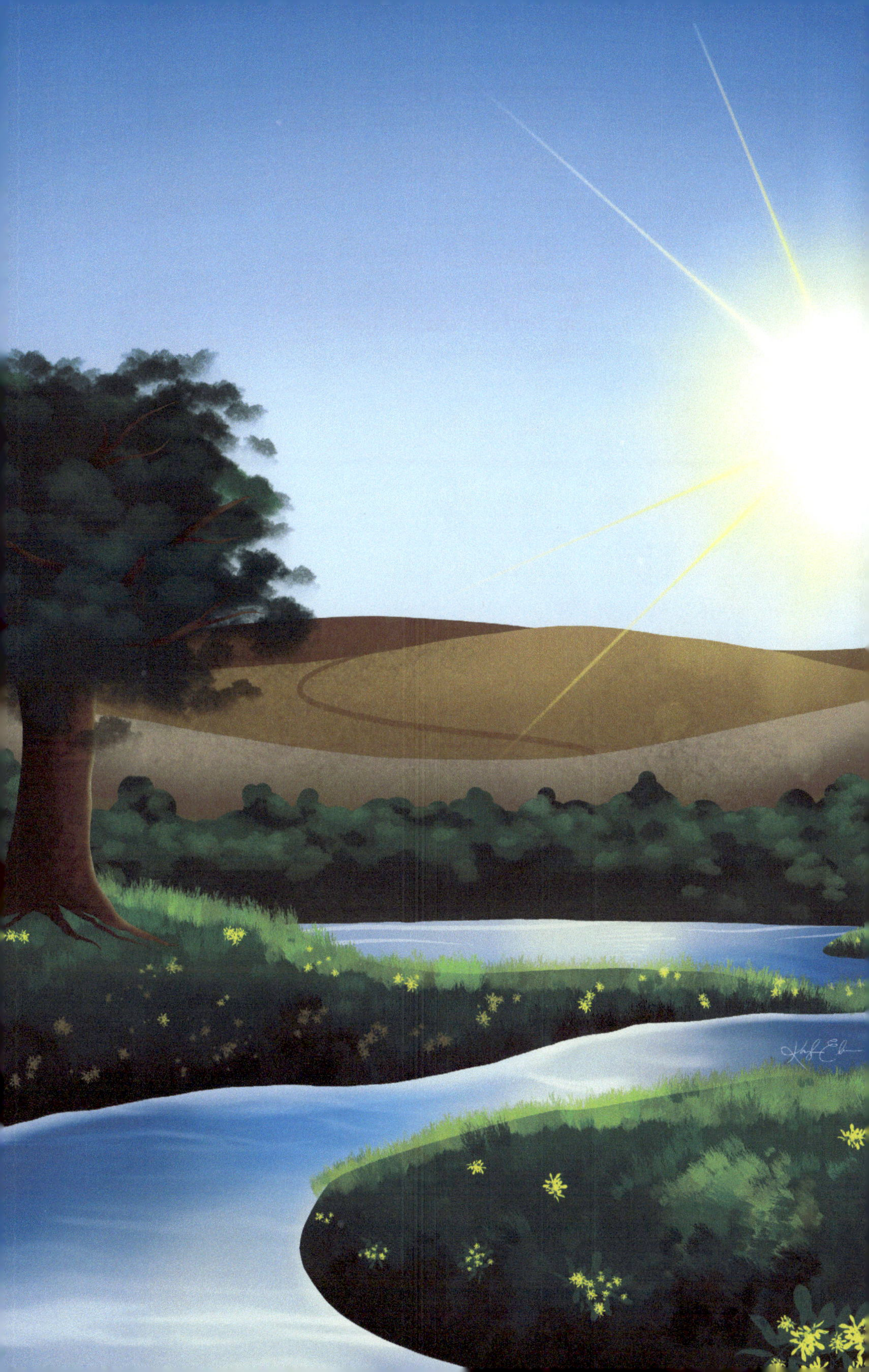

commonality

Talk to me, and you will see
that I am not all that different.
When given an opportunity
I've been taking the time to listen,
to be attentive.

Wiping the tears from my glasses, I see
that I am surrounded by weary warriors,
struggling just like me.
Struggling just to be,
struggling to resist and exist,
to be set free.

But we
will emerge victorious.
Though our journeys may not be so glorious,
I am urging you to be courageous.
Cheering you on,
we will support each other in these
emotional marathons.

Because, that's what true friends are for.
And the more I ponder and pay attention,
I find that I **always** had many more.

(1 Peter 5:9, Proverbs 17:17) *NWT*

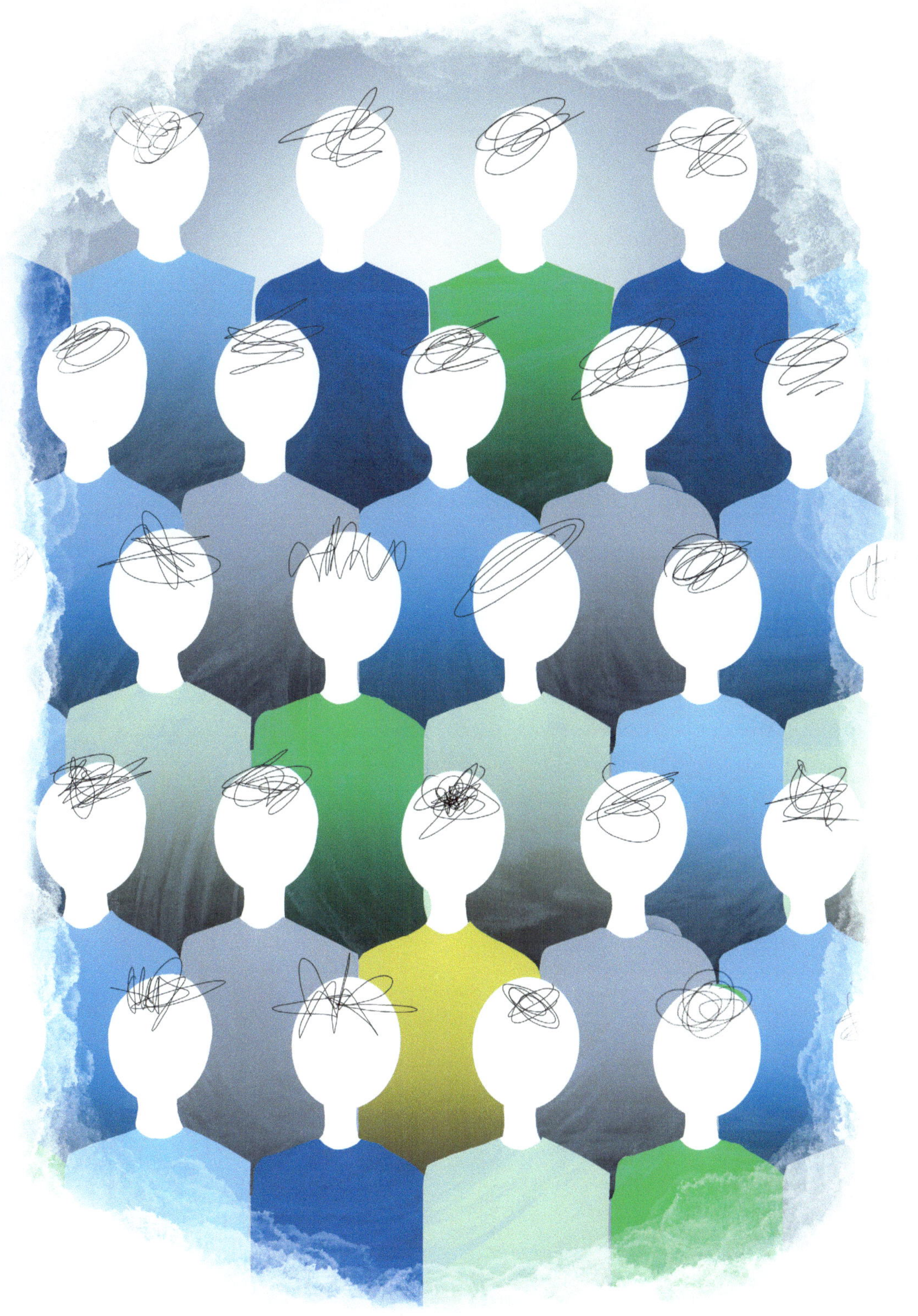

gravity

I'm taking a moment to say, thank you
for all that you do.
Expressing appreciation, admiration
for the way you pulled through.
If only I could have warned you,
that entering into my stratosphere
would be so catastrophic.
If I had known healthier coping skills
then maybe I could have stopped it.
When I was feeling overwhelmed
I'd reach a higher attitude—I mean altitude.
Still, you found a way to reach me,
mapping my latitude and my longitude.
Admissions became emissions
turning the air around me into hazardous conditions.
If only I could have just warned you
of the astronomical pressure I was under.
My barometer was broken,
I had no means to measure, I was blundered.
Maybe then you could have been more prepared,
better equipped.
Maybe at least then, you could have just dipped.
But no,
you rose to the challenge.
You learned to discern my triggers
and recenter my balance.
Studying my universe,
you've become quite versed
in sorting through the wild talk,
and in kissing where it hurts.
In dodging the meteor showers
to assure me of my power.
In always finding a way to show up
in the final hour.

My heart clings to all those precious moments
when you couldn't have been any sweeter.
If only I could have warned you.
But I didn't know either.

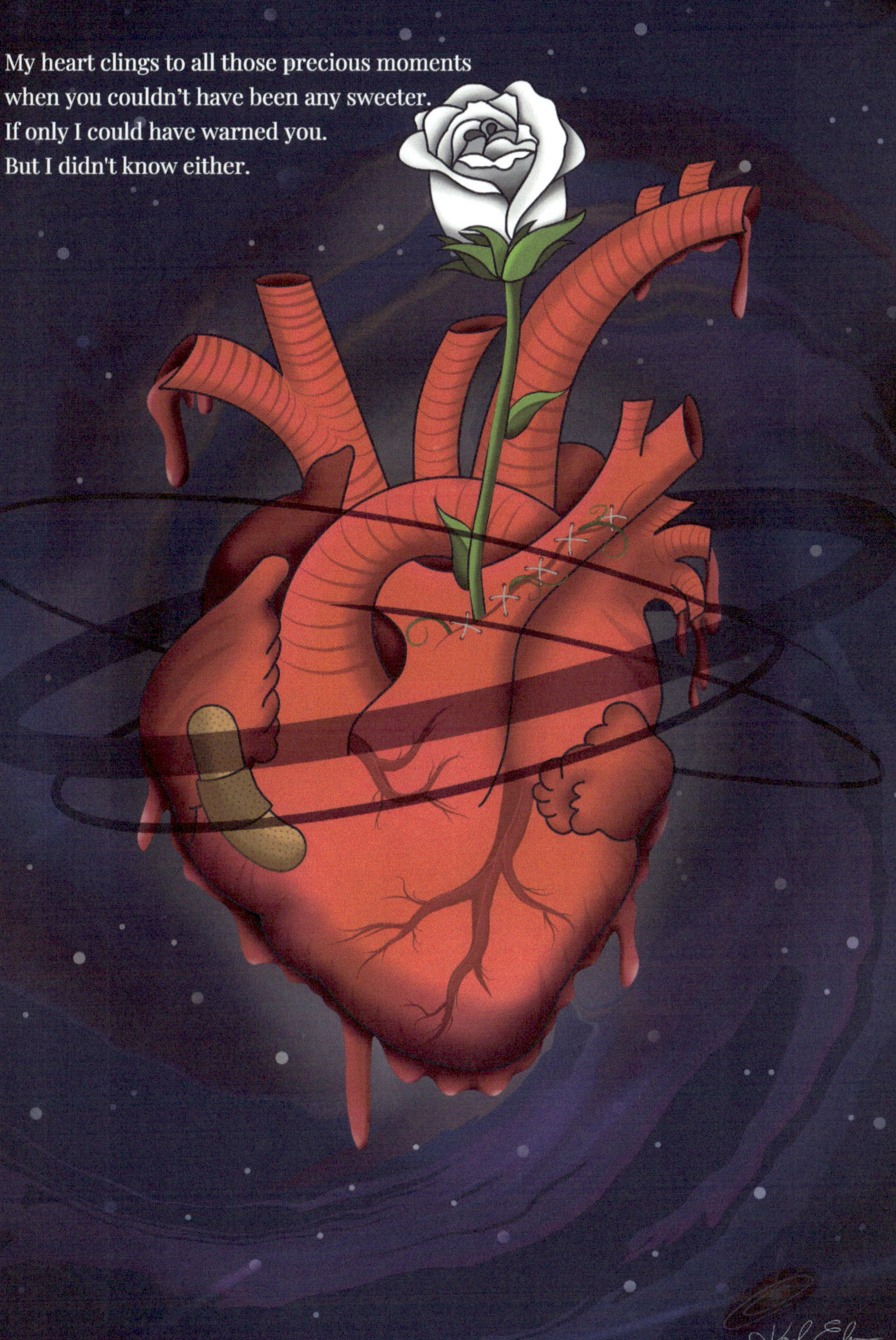

my eternal friend

At times I might feel,
w o r t h l e s s .
Like, "Life can't get any worse than this."
But then, he reminds me of my purpose.
Rekindling my zeal, leaving me fired and focused.

Endless days of senseless mistakes.
Countless flurries of insanity.
Just as I appear to be taking shape,
meaningless bouts of earthly vanity.
Somehow he always vouched for me.

Sometimes, I feel I don't deserve him.
Like, "Surely, there's someone so much better."
Yet, he reassures me of my value,
nonetheless, I am a debtor.
But who isn't?

Still, he loves me all the same.
He was there when I was broken,
my heart, riddled with shame.
He's watched me struggle through my ignorance,
his wealth of wisdom sheltering my domain.

Now, I am certain he is my strength,
and soon *all* will know his name.
My best friend, my rock, my comfort.
There is no one greater.
With him, I could never be outnumbered.

He is l o v e.

(1 John 4:16) *NWT*

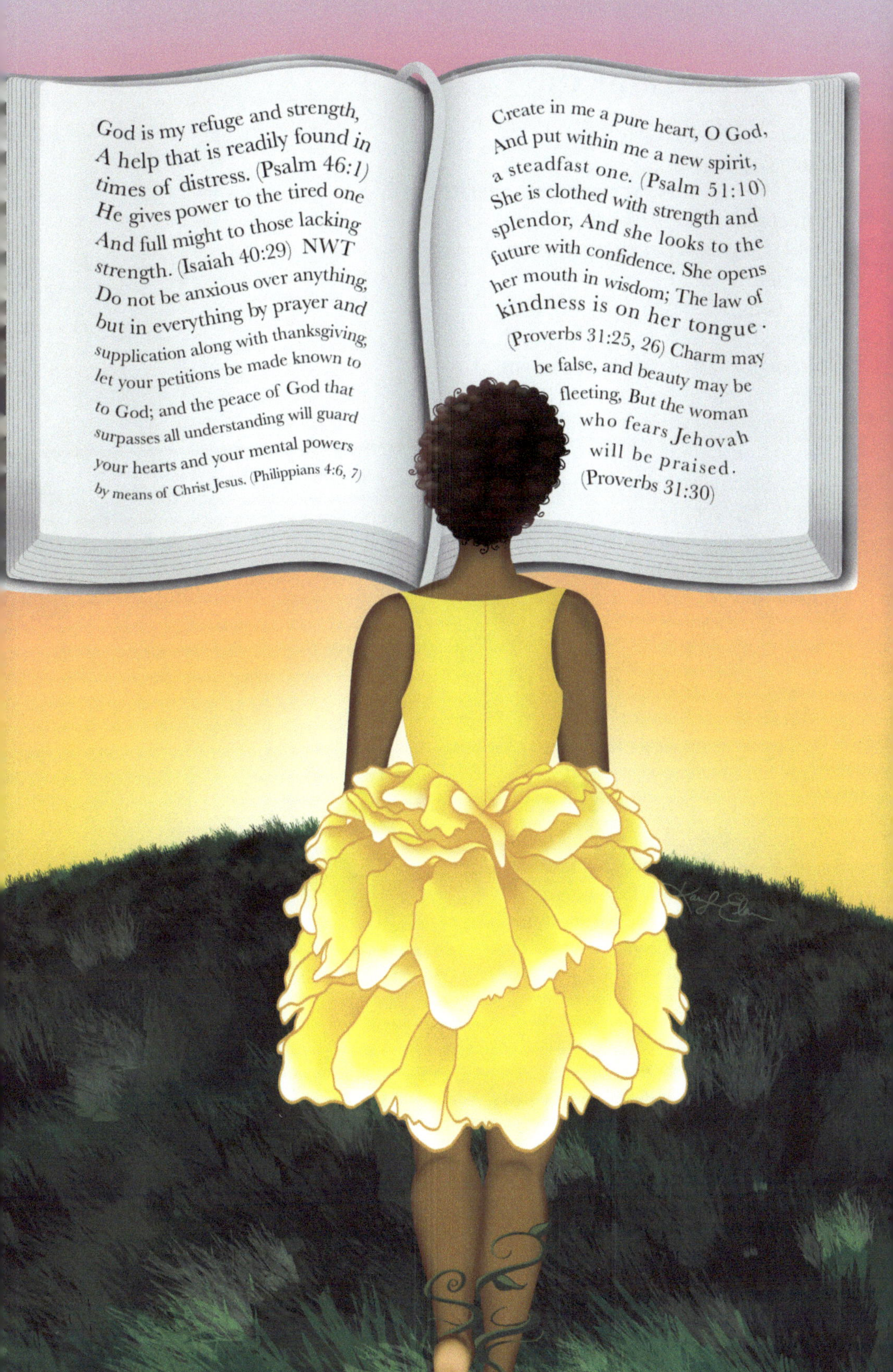
God is my refuge and strength,
A help that is readily found in
times of distress. (Psalm 46:1)
He gives power to the tired one
And full might to those lacking
strength. (Isaiah 40:29) NWT
Do not be anxious over anything,
but in everything by prayer and
supplication along with thanksgiving,
let your petitions be made known to
to God; and the peace of God that
surpasses all understanding will guard
your hearts and your mental powers
by means of Christ Jesus. (Philippians 4:6, 7)
Create in me a pure heart, O God,
And put within me a new spirit,
a steadfast one. (Psalm 51:10)
She is clothed with strength and
splendor, And she looks to the
future with confidence. She opens
her mouth in wisdom; The law of
kindness is on her tongue.
(Proverbs 31:25, 26) Charm may
be false, and beauty may be
fleeting, But the woman
who fears Jehovah
will be praised.
(Proverbs 31:30)

cause and affect

It's more than safe to say that
focusing on you
was the only way I'd see it through.
The only reason I'm still alive,
why my yellow's no longer blue.
Remembering
the faculties beyond my tiny being.
Remembering that I am loved, that I am seen.
When anxieties weigh me down
it is to you I cling.
Bring me back down to earth.
Your Voice comforts me,
soothes my wounds from the hurt.
Your love grounds me
anchors me deep within the dirt.
When negative thoughts attack my peace
only to you I revert.

You cause to become
my refuge from the storm.
You cause to become
my energy, empowering me to go on.
You cause to become
my strength, when these burdens are hard to bear.
You cause to become
my sanity, granting me peace beyond compare.
You cause to become
my father, protecting me from distress.
You cause to become
my wisdom, guiding me to success.
You cause to become
my light, illuminating my path.
You cause to become
my hope, the greatest one could ever have.

You cause to become
my joy, that I am demanding back
and this time, I will not let it slip away.
No, *this* time
my joy is here to stay.

(Philippians 4:13, Exodus 3:14) *NWT*

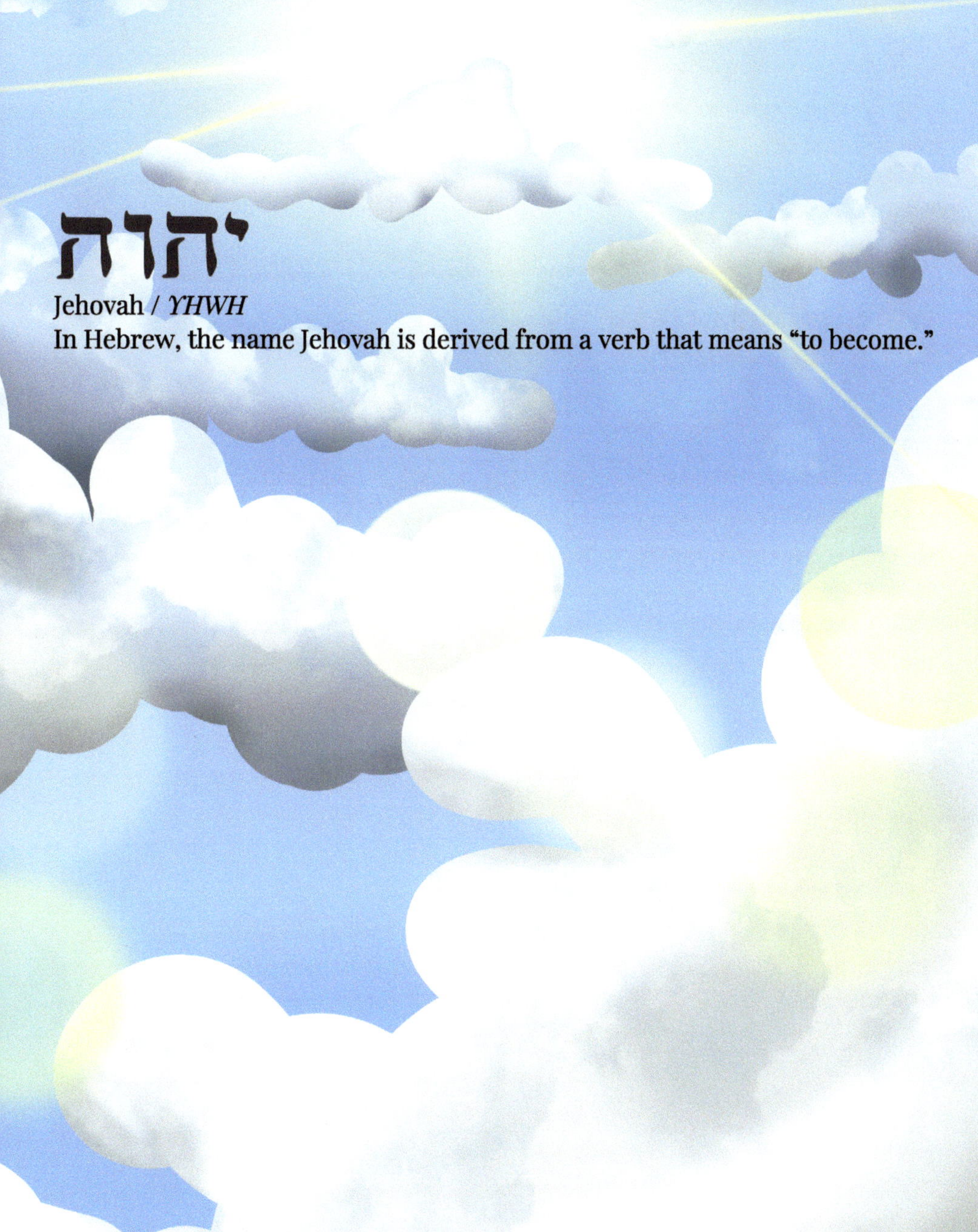

יהוה

Jehovah / *YHWH*

In Hebrew, the name Jehovah is derived from a verb that means “to become.”

reality check

Did I break?
Yes.

Was it pretty?
No.

Is it mendable?
Yes.

Will it be easy?
No.

But will I be better for it?
Yes.

I am no less
of a person because I battle depression.

It is that very pang of distress,
that struggle, that imperfection

that makes me
human.

(James 3:2) *NWT*

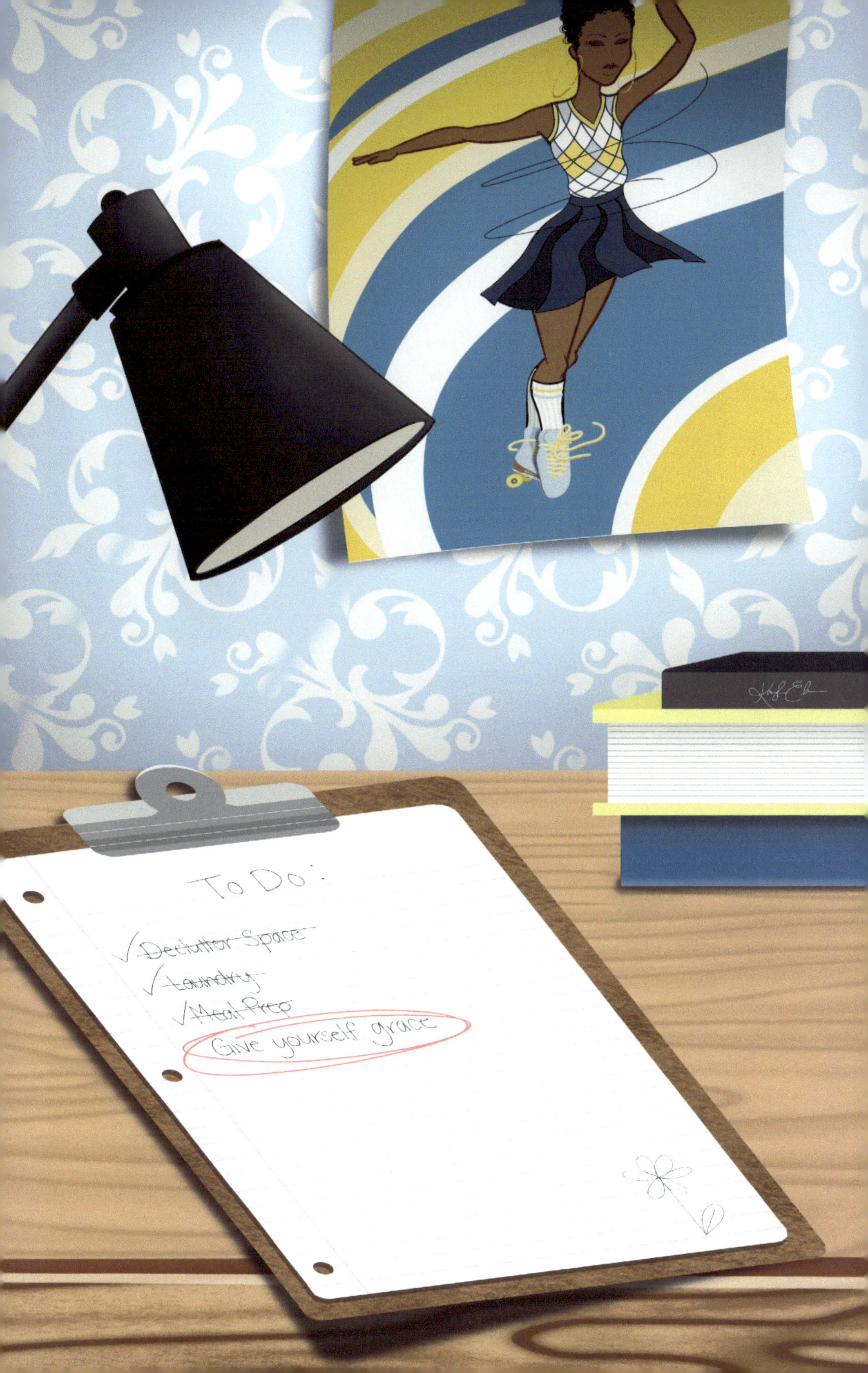
To Do:
~~Declutter Space~~
~~Laundry~~
~~Meal Prep~~
Give yourself grace

a pantoum of affirmation

Depression will not overtake me
because I am creating my own safety.
I am whole, and I am complete
regardless of anxiety.

Because I am creating my own safety
there is no need for escape, you see.
Regardless of anxiety,
my confidence is replete.

There is no need for escape. See,
depression will not overtake me.
My confidence is replete,
I am whole, and I am complete.

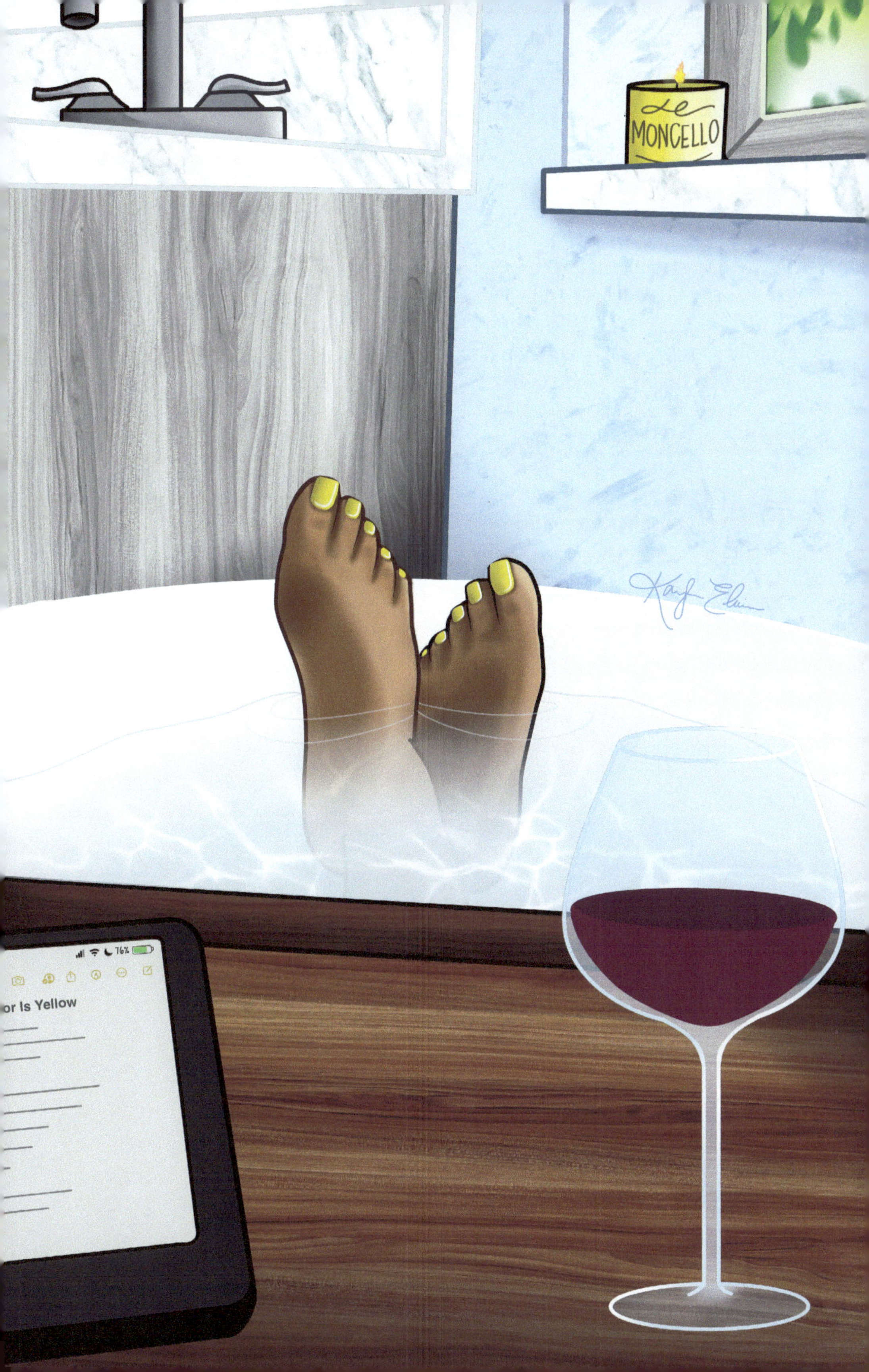
MONCELLO
76%
or Is Yellow

strong

I am strong.
Not because I am a woman.
Not because I am black.
Not because I am a "strong black woman."
No, I am strong because I choose to be.
I am strong because Jah chooses me.
I am strong because I bolster my will and forge
ever forward in whichever way God uses me.
Strong is refusing to revert back to who I used to be.
I am strong because when I lack,
I double back, to pick up all of the tiny little pieces
that have fallen through the cracks.
See, *that's* what strong is.
I am strong because I am diligent.
I am determined.
I am strong because even when the odds were stacked
against me, I took the cards that I was dealt
and I shuffled,
and I shuffled,
and I shuffled my viewpoint until my vantage excelled.
I am strong, because in my vulnerability
I gained the tools required to build from where I failed.

I am strong;

because even when my own mind tries to convince me that I am not,

I tell it
it's wrong.

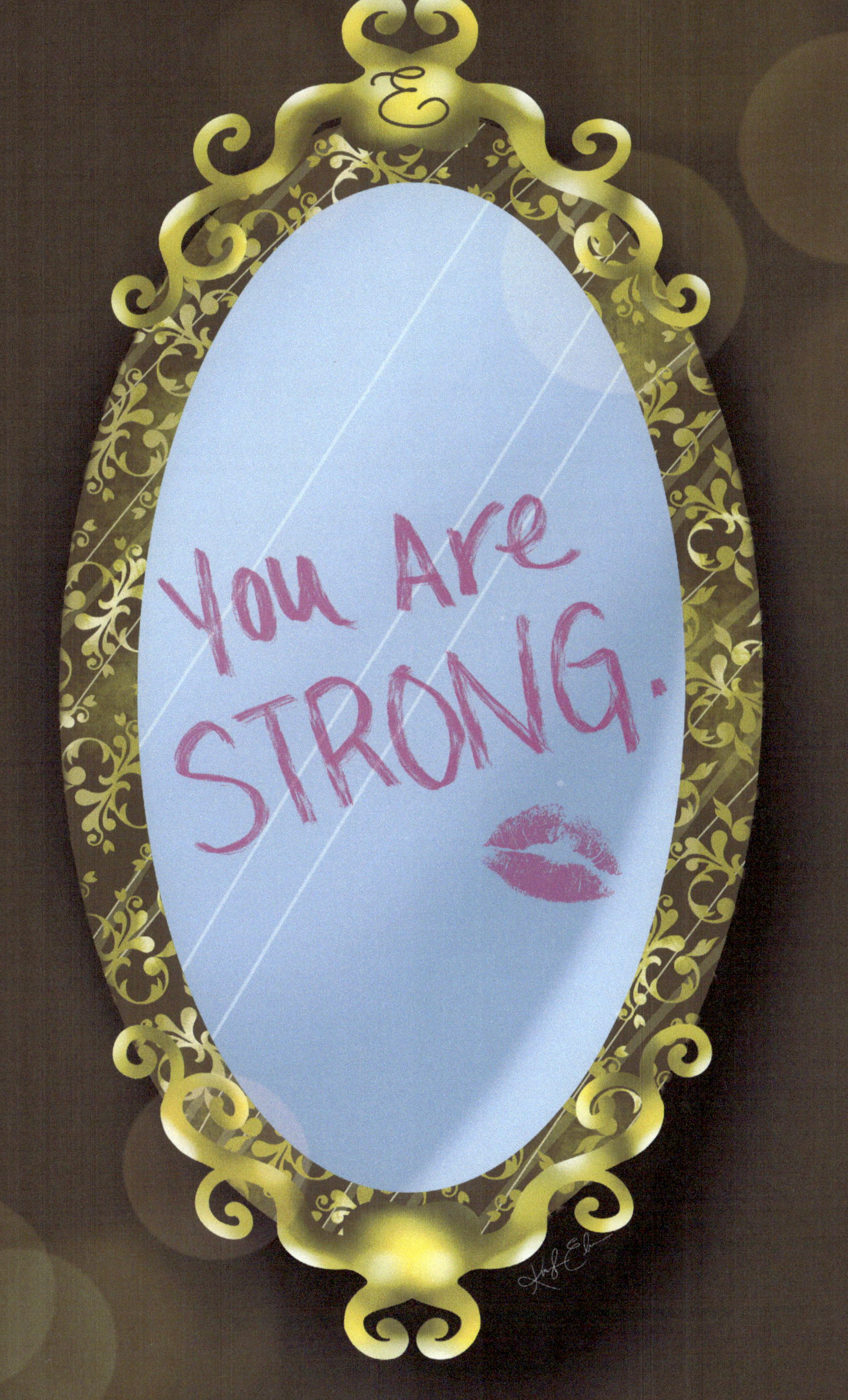
You Are
STRONG.

marigold

I am stretching my stem
as if to catch the sun with my face;
and when it rains I am resilient,
my shoot springing back with grace.

I am a wise young flower, and I'm growing every day.
Picking at my petals, and learning along the way.
I'm learning to, learn myself. Discovering that mistakes are okay.
Fighting to stand firm against the tumultuous winds that sway.

I am rooted in the richest of soil, but not in terms of wealth.
I mean in terms of love and wisdom, of spiritual health.
I mean that I was sought,
that I am cherished, I am taught.

I am grateful to be grounded in a way that some are not.
Some tulips are neglected,
some lilies wither and wry,
some roses "have it all" but rot from the inside.

At times, the air amidst my fragile bud may seem a bit too thick.
But in those moments, a gentle mind's whisper does the trick.
I am relieved, finally able to breathe.
Though I might struggle through the smog and blight
your presence never leaves.

So I continue in this journey with self-awareness, seeking growth.
Knowing that I am but one little flower within your scope.
I'm not a rose, nor a tulip, or even a lily,
yet I was chosen for your garden

and for *that*, I stand in hope.

(Colossians 2:6,7) *NWT*

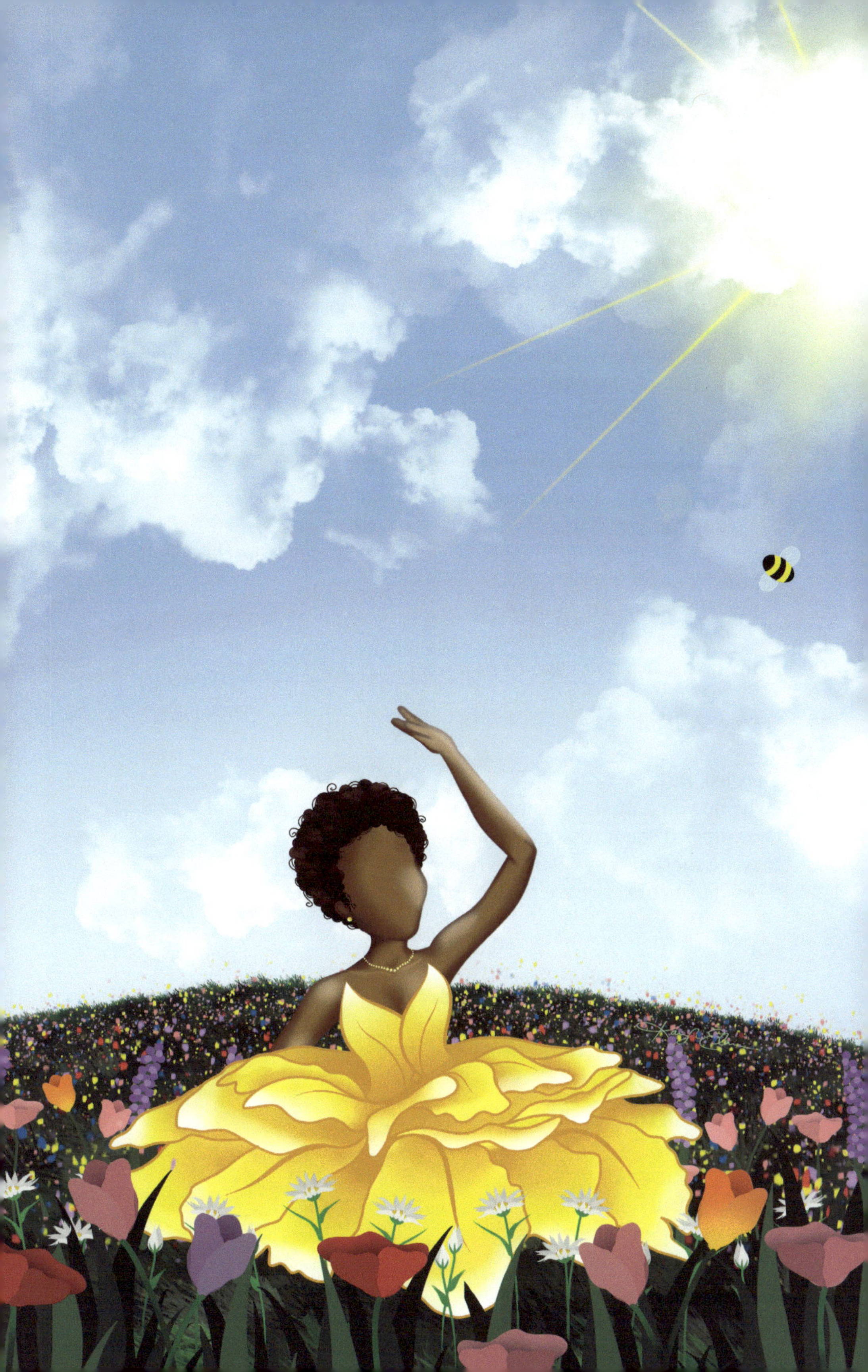

set me free

Set me free.
Put my emotions on display.
Relate all my disappointments
and tell about my dismay.

Set me free.
Put all my insecurities on blast,
and flood the minds of all your viewers
with painful memories from my past.

Set me free.
Run away with my fears.
Absorb the causes of my misery,
while dodging my tears.

Set me free.
Let people learn of my mistakes,
from trusting in the wrong people
to my facing heartbreaks.

Set me free.

They ask me,
"Why do you only write when you're mad?"
"Why does it seem you only glean
to write these things when you're sad?"
"Why do you always have to write all in your feelings so bad?"

But
what's a literary masterpiece
without the *grit*
of my catastrophe?
Without the *raw*
of pure emotion,
battered and fried in all my passion's grease?

I'm just tryna say,
You could call it crazy, but I find,
that pain and passion
fuels the pen in which I glide,
it sets me free.

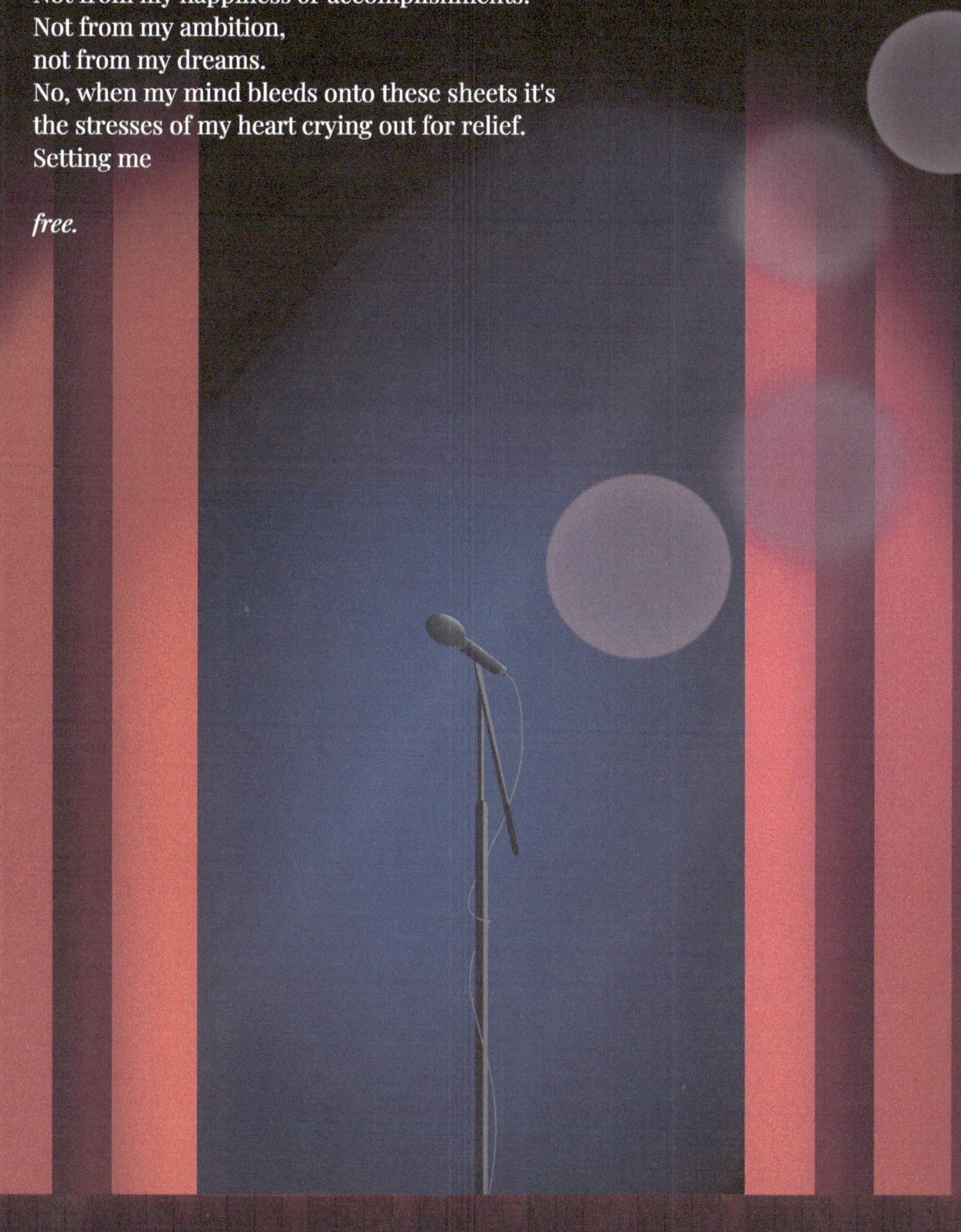
Not from my happiness or accomplishments.
Not from my ambition,
not from my dreams.
No, when my mind bleeds onto these sheets it's
the stresses of my heart crying out for relief.
Setting me

free.

my favorite color is yellow

REFERENCES

Mayo Clinic Staff. (October 20, 2022) *Depression (major depressive disorder)*

https://www.mayoclinic.org/diseases-conditions/depression/symptoms-causes/syc-20356007?utm_source=Google&utm_medium=abstract&utm_content=Major-depression&utm_campaign=Knowledge-panel

Guirguis, Monica. (June 19, 2020) *Stress vs. Clinical Anxiety and How to Spot the Difference.* https://www.arnoldpalmerhospital.com/content-hub/stress-vs-clinical-anxiety-and-how-to-spot-the-difference#:~:text=These%20are%20considered%20normal%20physiologic,or%20constant%20fear%20in%20general.

New World Translation of the Holy Scriptures. (NWT) Watch Tower Bible and Tract Society of Pennsylvania. 2013

https://www.jw.org/en/library/bible/study-bible/books/

Hood Life

Adulthood hit me hard.
Harder than any other hood I've met.
I mean like, the ‘j e c t s raised me,
You know, the streets were crazy.
Guns popped, sending bullets flying
while I strolled my plastic baby.
But no, it wasn't hard like this.

Time passed, leaving me involuntarily immersed
in the world of adolescence and that drama.
W o m a n h o o d .
Of course, everything that I had feared for came true.
You know, the boobies and blood stains foretold by Momma.
But no, it wasn't hard like this.

Along with that hood came the troubles of s i s t e r h o o d ,
like how I'm a girl, and she's a girl, but our two worlds clash.
Learning my place, who I am and what I rock with
wasn't something I did too fast.
But even still, it wasn't hard like this.
No. You see, a d u l t h o o d ,
hits hard with injustices.
Right hook to the jaw, it'll bust your lip.

All of a sudden,
I found myself entangled, in a variety of different choices;
from a career, to a relationship, establishing what my new voice is.
Because I had already “found myself,” back when I was 16.
But now, it’s almost like a new character's on the screen.
I mean, same movie, but it switched to a different scene.
You know that one part, with the plot twist
that like, no one could have ever seen?
That's a d u l t h o o d .

And of course it doesn't end there.
I have to keep my focus, *focused*
but it's hard to breathe in thin air.
My atmosphere has become cluttered
by the stresses of real life.
As well as the joys of good times and meeting Mr. Right.

I think. But that's the thing, you can never be too certain.
You start overthinking about whether or not
the choices you make could leave somebody hurting.
Him, her, or even yourself—
and the trickiest part of it all is
trying to overcome these things in stealth.
That's a d u l t h o o d .

kayla eloise | 2017

—

This was one of the first poems ever to be shared publicly. I had always been proud of my work but I never imagined it might be good enough to be appreciated by others. When I shared this poem at a talent showcase, the response was surreal. I was so overwhelmed by the love and support shown to me. It truly validated my skill for this craft and motivated me to keep going.

Thank *you* for your support, and for believing in me too.

www.ingramcontent.com/pod-product-compliance
Lightning Source LLC
LaVergne TN
LVHW052308100826
845147LV00006B/705

* 9 7 9 8 2 1 8 9 6 7 0 9 3 *